Modern EdTech Leadership

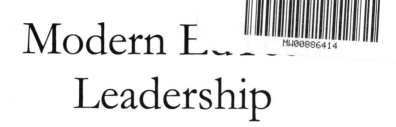

Mike Daugherty

Copyright © 2020 **Mike Daugherty**

All rights reserved.

ISBN: **9781521767221**

ISBN: **9781521767221**

CONTENTS

ACKNOWLEDGMENTS

I have to start by thanking my awesome wife, Megan, for listening to me blather on about edtech ideals when all we both really want to do is watch football. Thank you for all your listening and support.

Many of the ideas outlined in this book come from my own personal experiences through twenty years of edtech leadership. Individuals such as Doug Jones, Nitin Julka, Paul Doxsey, and countless others contributed to those experiences along the way. Thank you for being a part of the endless planning sessions, conversations, and experiments that culminated in this publication.

FOREWORD

The traditional role of the school district technology director has become obsolete. Speak with your average teacher in many school districts across the nation, and you'll find the perception of many staff members is that the technology department is better known for getting in the way and causing roadblocks than for serving the vast educational needs of both students and staff. In 2015, we see a rigid dichotomy between the traditional mindset of school district technology leaders and those leaders and teams who have shifted to a mindset that puts students - not technology - at the center of organizational decision-making.

Having the opportunity to lead the Future Ready effort, and through my team's work in running Digital Learning Day, I have the opportunity to work with over a thousand district leaders each year on digital learning implementation and systemic transformation. In our current educational landscape, there is often a complete disconnect between departments and school district leaders when it comes to various aspects of a digital conversion. Quite often, districts fall into the trap of purchasing hundreds, if not thousands of devices, putting them in carts and classrooms across the district, and then a short time later find themselves asking, "now what?" Simply put, purchasing the devices and deploying them, although time consuming on a large scale, is the easy part. Systematically shifting instructional pedagogy in the classroom, and supporting the needs of diverse learners, is the hard part; but **the part that matters most.** School district technology leaders that are creating such cultures of innovation in their districts have a clear vision of student-centered, technology-infused, personalized learning, with a comprehensive plan of implementation. These action plans include a myriad of interconnected areas
such as; curriculum, instruction, and assessment; professional learning; community engagement; data and privacy; the use of time; budget and resources; technology, networks, and

hardware; and the dynamic leadership and culture to make it all possible.

Technology leaders navigating this transformation are redefining traditional methodologies and closing gaps; gaps that cause teacher frustration and inadvertently impede student learning. Such gaps include, but are not limited to;

The Communication Gap
Poor communication builds frustration, confusion, and when significant enough, can cause organizational mistrust. Leaders finding success in closing this gap have a staff that is responsive, detail-oriented, leverage various communication tools, and are strategic in their messaging and communication methods.

The Innovation Gap
School technology leaders working to create a culture of innovation build trust among staff, promote risk-taking, provide adequate access to digital devices and tools, don't adhere to the "lock it and block it" mentality, are timely and efficient in meeting needs, move from acceptable to responsible use, and provide a feedback model that leverages both teacher and student voice.

The Equity Gap
As digital resources increase, so too can the digital divide - both in terms of access and infusion by staff. District technology leaders closing this gap do whatever it takes to ensure adequate levels of connectivity for all students, problem solve to support students without access at home, and meet the need for anytime, anywhere learning for both students and staff.

The Mindset Gap
Closing the mindset gap is not an easy feat, but one that is vital to sustainable change. Technology leaders having success in this area prioritize personalized professional learning opportunities for their team, model expectations, leverage

success stories and already established pockets of innovation, shift terminology from "you and them" to "we and our", spend adequate time in classrooms to understand instructional needs, and most importantly, put students at the heart of all decision-making.

The Relationship Gap

Relationships are the heart of transformation. District technology teams closing the relationship gap value people - their human capital and best asset, and work tirelessly to build a culture of trust and respect, showing all members of the team that they matter. These leaders understand that together we are better for the children that we serve.

This book, Modern EdTech Leadership, has been specifically written to support the transformation of school technology leaders and their teams. As designed, this book will push the thinking of these teams, while simultaneously providing insight into how to close key gaps, so that they can be the foundation of a dynamic digital conversion, working to better meet the needs of the students and staff that they serve. Throughout the book, Daugherty lays out a roadmap filled with both sound and practical advice on leading a technology team that supports high quality teaching and learning by providing students and staff with the tools, resources, and supports needed to better prepare students for their tomorrow.

How will you lead? The choice is up to you.

All for the kids we serve,
Thomas C. Murray
State and District Digital Learning Director
Alliance for Excellent Education, Washington, DC
thomascmurray.com | @thomascmurray

1
Times Are a Changin'

Public education is in the midst of a revolution. Disruptive
innovation is changing the way teachers teach and students
learn. Our students live in a digital world, altered by ever-
changing technology. Whether they are described as "Digital
Natives" or "21st Century Learners," it is evident to everyone in
public education that students today are very different from
those of years past. School districts need to embrace the
changes brought on by advancements in technology to stay
relevant. Sir Ken Robinson, a renowned author and
educational theory expert, discussed the overwhelming need
for a change in the way public education operates in his 2010
TED talk titled "Changing Education Paradigms." In that talk, he
states, "The problem is that the current system of education
was designed and conceived and structured for a different
age." He's absolutely right. The classrooms our students are
using now, look very similar to the classroom their parents and
even their grandparents used. Sir Ken Robinson believes that
the current educational system in the United States promotes

standardization and conformity instead of an individualized, creative approach to education.

Clayton M. Christensen, Professor of Business Administration at Harvard Business School, founded the Institute for Disruptive Innovation in 2010. The goal of his organization is to "improve the world through disruptive innovation." One of the institute's main concentrations is education, specifically looking at how online learning affects schools and universities across the nation.

Ideas such as blended learning, flipped classrooms, personalized learning, and 1:1 computing have taken center stage in this upheaval of traditional learning environments. When you look at those terms, there is one underlying theme that becomes apparent. All of these ideas rely on access. Access to technology and access to the Internet, yet every day in this country, millions of students are affected by ineffective technology departments that don't see this shift. If you don't believe me, ask five of your friends how they feel about the technology or the technical support staff in their district. I can almost guarantee you that at least two of those friends will not have positive things to say about their IT department. Students and staff lose countless instructional hours due to a lack of planning and inefficient operations on the part of the tech department.

A technology director's role within a school district is rapidly changing, but many individuals in this role do not seem to comprehend this premise. People talk about the "haves" and the "have nots." When I think about individuals in technology leadership roles, I classify them as the "wills" and the "will nots." The "wills" group encompasses those who understand their role in the revolution that K-12 is experiencing. They will make student-centered decisions, even if those decisions are difficult. They will provide access to devices, sites, tweets, videos, and information students need to learn, grow, and compete globally. They will be an agent of change in their district.

The "will nots," on the other hand, are doomed. These individuals will not embrace new technologies but will continue to cling to what has worked in the past. By doing what they've always done, they'll inevitably hold their district back. These once brilliant directors will no longer lead the revolution; they will stifle it. The saddest part is that most will not even realize their faults. They will be proud of their work. The day will come when the district will choose to move forward without them, either through attrition or reduction in force. They will be left wondering how they arrived at such an unwanted end.

Further validation of this idea can be seen in hiring non-traditional technical people to lead the district's IT department. The "will not" mentality results in little to no growth of technology implementation in the classroom. Teachers become frustrated. This frustration causes the district leadership to question the technology leadership. Districts need an individual that understands more than just technology in order to move forward. They need someone who understands education and the role that technology plays in academia. They need someone who can communicate on their level. Someone who can handle talking to a room full of their peers with confidence. There is a growing trend to hire a teacher to lead the technology department instead of a traditional tech person. They want someone who "gets education" even if they are not the most tech-savvy person in the room. I've asked the same question in almost every presentation I've given to CTOs in the last few years: "How many of you in this room are former educators?". The number of raised hands continues to climb. Don't believe me? Look at the ten most recent hires in the districts that are close to you. I'd be willing to bet that at least three of the ten have an education background.

The old school mindset would suggest that someone lacking a technical background cannot lead the department. What about the switches, servers, and other digital aspects that do require that deeper understanding? Districts can look to employ a network engineer to handle the technical details. Advances in technology over the last ten years have decreased the need for an onsite engineer, especially in smaller districts. In those scenarios, districts purchase a block of hours with a consulting group to manage and maintain the network infrastructure.

Depending on what side of that fence you fall on, you may read portions of this text with which you disagree. You may have dealt with the same scenario presented and felt the experience was different overall. You may view these ideas as senseless. As you read these words, please be conscious that these are ideas, strategies, and designs that have been successful for me. It doesn't mean they are perfect or represent every possible way to handle a situation. I am fully aware that every district and every team is different. Use this book as a guide and apply the techniques that best fit your circumstances.

I've grown in many aspects as an educational technology since the original version of this book was released in 2015. One of the more profound changes was the discovery of COSN and the "Framework of Essential Skills of the K-12 CTO".

The Framework of Essential Skills of the K-12 CTO comprises three primary professional categories in the education technology field. Each of these categories includes ten essential skill areas, outlining the responsibilities and knowledge needed to be a viable educational technology leader.   I have personally used the framework to validate the ideas described in this text and grow in my CTO role. The revised version you're reading now incorporates COSN's philosophies with my own.

Along with the framework of essential skills, COSN created the Certified Education Technology Leader (CETL) certification. Obtaining this accreditation lets the world know that you have the skills required to lead K-12 organizations into the future. It's a validation of your skillset. In November of 2020, I published Certified Edtech Leadership. (https://bit.ly/CertEdTech) which take a deep dive into the ideas of COSN and ISTE as it relates to educational technology leadership. It also serves as a study guide for the CETL certification if that is something you wish to pursue.

The truth is that with proper planning, communication systems, and authentic customer service, almost any IT department can be successful. This book is a guide to mastering the art of technical support in the K-12 environment. You can expect to learn the steps necessary to take your department to the next level, regardless of your role in the department. I've spent close to twenty years in the education industry, many of them as a desktop technician, network administrator, or in a similar support position. While I have since graduated to an administrative role, this book was written with years of experience in all related positions being kept in mind. Technicians can use the concepts to help advance their careers. Administrators will learn how to approach their role from a different perspective, not merely a technical one. You can start using strategies immediately that will lead to a radical change in the perception of the technology team.

2
Interviews & Hiring

When designing a successful technology department, the goal should be to build a team of individuals who can support the district stakeholders with confidence, personality, and patience. These are the skills you want every member of your team to possess.

For starters, every member of the department should be confident in their ability to solve a problem. When he/she is working with a staff member, that individual expects the support personnel to know how to resolve the issue. There are billions of snags when it comes to technology. Expecting one person to be fluent in all of them is absurd, but this does not seem to concern most end users. Most want a 'fix' from the technology expert that will correct whatever issue they seem to be having at the time.

A former supervisor once told me that in a tech support role, you should never tell someone, "I don't know the answer." It shows "weakness" in the technician or the organization. In my travels, I've spoken to several people who believe in this philosophy. In my opinion, this is a terrible way to view and handle support. As a technician, this puts you in a very awkward spot. When asked a support question that you do not have the answer to, this method pushes you to lie to the individual(s) you are trying to assist. As an alternative, I offer up this suggested response:

"Honestly, I've never dealt with this particular issue, but I am confident I can get this resolved for you."

A reply similar to the one above shows the end-user that you are human and don't know everything. There's an authenticity that comes into play when openly admitting you do not have the answer. In my experience, this also creates a connection between the two people because you are showing them you are both in the same boat. Neither one of you know the answer, but you are willing to do the work to get it resolved. Fortunately for us, we live in an age where access to information is quickly available. When presented with a problem we have never seen before, we can use that access to discover others who have dealt with similar issues. We can use the knowledge available to solve whatever headache is plaguing the person standing in the doorway.

The bottom line is this: Technology skills are excellent, but an authentic, likable personality is much more desirable. Tech skills can be taught, but authenticity cannot. Let's explore how you can build a team of technicians that possess both the tech skills and the personality needed to master the art of IT support in the K-12 environment.

Interviewing
Hiring a new employee can be difficult, especially for a smaller district. Depending on its employees' turnover rate, a school system may only look for a new IT staff member every few years. In other scenarios, the turnover rate is very high, which results in new hires every few months. Regardless of how often you need to make a hiring decision, it is not a task that should be taken lightly. Plain and simple, you need the right people on your team to be successful.

Reviewing Resumes

A candidate's resume is a small window into their professional experience. It needs to make enough of a first impression on the hiring manager to consider devoting time to speak to the applicant. It should be polished, perfected. It is one of the only ways to stand out against the countless others vying for this position.

When reviewing a stack of resumes for an IT position, there are a few noteworthy items:

- **Spelling / Grammatical Errors** - These are a personal pet peeve of mine. Mistakes on a resume lead me to believe the candidate did not take his/her time to review their work thoroughly. While I am not a grammatical master in any way, I am smart enough to know the importance of a well-polished resume. Candidates can quickly address spelling errors or grammatical mistakes through careful proofreading, collaboration with others, and clicking "Check Spelling" before submitting to a potential employer.

- **Incorrect Software Names** – In an attempt to pad their resume, the applicant includes a software package that doesn't exist—for example, Microsoft Office 2012. Microsoft has Server 2012, but not Office. Mistakes like this happen much more than one might expect. When I see this, I immediately pass on the applicant. It's perfectly normal to embellish a bit on your resume, but make sure you know what you are talking about first. I touch on how to deal with resume padding later in the interview section of this chapter.

- **Previous Experience In a Service Profession** – In my experience, I've found success in those who have worked a job whose compensation relies heavily on tips, such as a waiter or waitress. To make more money, you have to understand what it takes to keep a customer satisfied. One must learn to adapt very quickly based on how each situation unfolds. That is a great skill to bring to the table for a career in IT.

Pre-Interview

There are a few details I look for when the candidate arrives at the interview. In my mind, these are subtle details that give you great insights into the applicant.

- **Dress Code** – Someone looking for my approval for employment should show up dressed accordingly, regardless of the position for which they are applying. My personal preference is a suit and tie. With that being said, I understand that some folks, such as recent graduates, don't necessarily own a suit. A dress shirt and tie is acceptable. When a candidate shows up in more casual clothing, it says they are not serious about the position or have a potential issue with authority.

- **Notebook** – When you attend a meeting of any kind, you should come prepared with a notebook, tablet, laptop, or some other way to record information. In my opinion, it is a sign of respect for the other people in attendance. It lets them know you value their time and what they have to say. In an interview, the applicant can expect quite a bit of information to come their way, so bringing something to capture that information shows forward-thinking and organizational skills.

The Actual Interview

As you conduct the interview, look for someone that can converse appropriately. Much of the IT industry is about fostering, growing, and maintaining relationships. If the applicant cannot hold a decent conversation with you, it is unlikely that they will converse well with staff daily. Technology skills can always be taught, but a personality should be well developed before an interview.

I am not suggesting that you hire someone with a great personality that has zero tech skills. You should have already passed over the people who did not have the skill set you were looking for when reviewing resumes. The point I am making is that communication is vital to success. The shy, stereotypical nerd that struggles when speaking to a real live human being is probably not the best option, regardless of his/her incredible technical knowledge.

There are nine questions that I believe will narrow the field down to two or three strong candidates during the interview itself. Typically these questions work better for entry-level positions; however, I have asked them when hiring network engineers, directors, and integrationists. Before starting with the questions, take a few minutes to give the candidate an overview of yourself, the company, and the position they are applying for. I like to explain precisely what the job entails, daily work life, and my expectations of the person in that role.

Phase 1: Planning and Critical Thinking

Question 1: Tell me a little about yourself and why you feel you would be a good fit for the position. The applicant should be able to give you some history on themselves as relevant to the work experience. The experience is essential, but I will dive into that in subsequent questions. The key to this question is the second half. You have explained to them what the position entails as well as your expectations. A strong candidate will connect their skill set back to those expectations.

Question 2 & 3: What would you consider is one of your strengths? What do you feel is your biggest weakness? On these two questions, I do not care too much about the content of the answer. I am looking for the person to have an answer prepared instead of sitting and thinking about it. These are two of the most common interview questions. You can find them in just about any interview prep guide. Having an answer primed for these shows me that the person prepared for the interview ahead of time.

Question 4: Where do you see yourself in 5 years?

You want someone who has a plan, not someone without any aspirations. Having someone without a goal means that they will probably be in that same position five years down the road if you hire them. That is fantastic for continuity, but it is improbable that someone like this will drive innovation or efficiency inside your organization. These people are stagnant. You want motivated individuals who will grow and encourage others to grow with them through their actions.

One candidate told me he hoped to have my role or a similar director-level position. While some people might find that presumptuous, I felt the exact opposite. I admired his willingness to be honest about where he wanted his future to go. Look for applicants that understand the importance of having a strategy for their career.

Question 5: What do you like to do in your spare time?

Over the years, I've found that the best technicians are the ones who are passionate about technology outside of their professional life. These are the people who tinker with computers when they have free time in the evenings or on weekends. They are attempting to set up a home media server, overclock their graphics card, or configure remote access to their home machine, which they may have custom-built from scratch.

Applicants like this devote some of their personal time to learning more about the tech that they love. From my experience, this leads to a shorter learning curve once hired. You will begin to see them make connections to the work they have done on their own and the tasks you are asking them to perform. Additionally, they are often self-taught. In my opinion, this individual is more likely to draw on his/her personal practices to develop out of the box solutions. For example, they will use a batch file, vb script, and a shared folder to resolve an access issue. It may not be the best practice, but in the end, it will probably work.

The only downside to a candidate that fiddles is they can fall into a trap where they are over-focused. They spend way too much time attempting to solve a problem, almost becoming blind to the time they have invested. In the end, they have spent 8 hours fixing an issue that could have just as easily been corrected with a $4.99 app. It's a behavior that is easily addressed as long as you are aware of the time invested.

Phase 2: Technical Ability / Customer Service
CTOs should tailor the next few questions to fit their district.

Question 6:   How comfortable are you with xx (Windows, servers, switches, imaging, etc).
I typically ask several questions along these same lines. I am looking to see if they have the technical knowledge that the position requires. When speaking with an applicant, use these questions to get a good feel of their skill level.

Avoid asking problem-specific questions, though. Here is an excellent example of a question that I received during an interview for a technical support role.

> "You're working on a Windows 7 machine in which the user has complained of a slow internet connection. What do you do?"

The person conducting the interview presented me with a recent problem from his company. That's a great idea, in theory. Ask the candidate to solve a real-world problem from the organization on the spot. The flaw in this grand idea is twofold.

There were so many other details that had not been provided for starters, which made answering the question difficult. For example, is this affecting everyone or just this user? Have other users with the same model device issued complaints as well? Is this a laptop that travels outside of the organization's firewall?

Since the interviewer focused on one specific answer, I was informed that no other information mattered when I pressed for additional details.

The other flaw is when a candidate's personal experience doesn't quite match up with the specific answer at hand. In this example, the correct answer was that I would update the network card drivers, which fixed the problem for his crew. Unfortunately for me, though, troubleshooting drivers was a rarity at my current position as our director had automated much of that process. Sure, I knew how to load new drivers, but I would have checked various other things before I went down that road.

I eventually got the question correct, but this question had disrupted the flow of an otherwise successful interview. I was unable to regain the momentum resulting in being passed over for the position. Naively, I offered up a similar scenario later in my career when I asked the questions. The result was the same as what I had experienced. In several roles after that, I've been asked to provide very detailed questions with specific answers to evaluate the applicant's troubleshooting skills. I refused this request time and again because I do not believe it provides any real value and can derail an interview.

Instead, I offer up question seven to address how an applicant troubleshoots an issue.

Question 7: Tell me about a technical issue that was a significant problem for your organization and how you solved it.

Through this question, the candidate gets the opportunity to describe a very challenging technical issue. We have all had those problems that are tough, but then once you solve them, you feel pretty damn good about yourself. You do not forget it either. That is the kind of story I look for here. It also helps to show their technical experience and troubleshooting methods. If they do not have an account like this, they may not have enough practical experience or rely on others to fix the larger issues.

Question 8: Test the resume BS meter

Most people pad their resumes. It is a common tactic. I would guess that as you are reading this, you are thinking about a few bullet points on your resume that are a bit overstated. I do not see anything wrong with this as long as you can confidently speak about the parts you have inflated. I like to ask a question or two about the elements of a resume that seem like they do not fit well or maybe a bit exaggerated. Like other questions I ask, I'm typically not interested in whether or not they possess the skill. I want to see how they respond to being called out on their embellishments.

The responses usually fall into three categories, all of which can give you insight into the type of person in front of you. In one scenario, the candidate has prepared for your questions and can speak fluently about the topic. This is my preferred course, mostly because I want to know the candidate has prepared ahead of time. The second possibility is that they fumble their words and ultimately admit to not knowing as much as they claimed. At first glance, this appears to be a significant interview mistake. However, if answered correctly, it does show that the applicant can admit to making a mistake. That is not an easy thing to do, especially during an interview. When this occurs, I watch to see if the person manages to recover on the next question.

Finally, there is my least desired response. Within just a few moments of the candidate discussing the topic at hand, it becomes apparent they do not know the subject matter. Instead of admitting that they overstated a skill set, they awkwardly babble on, hoping to convince you of their phantom abilities. The attempt to deceive is a major red flag and, in some cases, has wrecked an excellent interview up to that point. The ability to bullshit with others is an art form. When done correctly, it can be a considerable personality asset. When done poorly, though, others quickly see through your ruse, which leads to mistrust. If the person you are speaking to does not trust you, they will question everything you say. They will doubt your solutions to their problems, and you will become the person that "can't ever fix it right the first time." I rarely hire applicants that do not perform well on this question.

Question 9: What do you do when you don't know the answer to a problem?

What a simple question when you think about it. When working on a problem, what do you do when you do not know the answer? The answer is just as simple: Ask for help. Whether they ask a co-worker, manager, or a friend does not matter. The point is that the candidate understands that they will never know all the answers, and it's perfectly acceptable to ask someone for help. Why spend hours getting nowhere when the person who sits five feet away from you has dealt with that same issue hundreds of times in the past?

If this is an interview for a higher-level position, the answer should still be the same, in my opinion. Even in upper management roles, there is nothing wrong with reaching out to colleagues to collaborate on a solution. Think about your current position for a moment. When you are tasked with solving a particular problem, and you know someone who has already addressed this same issue, isn't your first instinct to call that person to learn more about how they resolved the issue in their organization? Even if their solution doesn't fit perfectly, it still gives a framework or reference point from which to work. It was not that long ago that I looked for a different response to this question. Initially, I wanted the applicant to say that they would use Google or YouTube to search for a resolution. If the applicant responds that they would start with search engines or YouTube, agree with their logic, but then rephrase the question to include exploring both options without success. Where would you go for help if you'd already searched online with limited success?

Question 10: Let's say you are walking down the hall with a list of tickets in your hand. A teacher pops her head out and says,

"Oh hey, tech guy. Glad you're here. I am having trouble with my laptop. Can you help really quick?" The teacher does not have a ticket in the system. What do you do?

A potential employer asked this to me years ago, and I have asked it many times myself. In my opinion, the correct answer is that you'll stop and quickly assess the issue. If it's a five-minute fix, you do it on the spot and ask the teacher to throw in a ticket later so you can get it in the books. If it's not going to be a quick fix, you tell the user, "This issue is going to require a bit more time than I have available right now. Can you please place a work order? Someone will be out as soon as possible".

The goal is to satisfy the teacher as much as possible, but not forget that he/she did not follow the procedure. You came here to do tickets that others correctly placed. They should have priority because they were in the queue first. If it is a quick fix, everyone wins. If not, you have still provided him/her a path to resolution.

Summary
I often talk to entry-level technicians about the moment that everything finally clicks for them. There's an enlightenment that occurs. It is the point in time when they stop relying on guesswork and past experiences. This event finally connects all the technical dots for the technician.

Like many seasoned technicians, I remember when this happened to me. A ticket came in about inconsistent network connectivity issues on a PC. I was confident in my abilities, so after just a few troubleshooting, I threw the OSI model's seven layers right out the window. I had seen PCs struggle with network connectivity before. I grabbed all the tricks in my bag and began working. I hardcoded the IP to eliminate DHCP, flushed the DNS cache, ran multiple virus scans, and reloaded the network driver. Nothing I tried helped with the issue at hand. Not to be deterred, I dug further. I hit up Google and began focusing on server related issues, even mentioning to a colleague that I thought it might be a sign of broader network issues.

At this point, I had spent close to two and a half hours troubleshooting a network connectivity issue on a PC. I was beginning to think that Windows had become corrupt based on countless tech support forum threads. When I started to disconnect the machine to take it back to my Office to be reimaged, the network cable fell out of the wall. The problem was nothing more than a loose wire. All that time for a thirty-second fix. The moment that yellow network cable hit the office floor was the point that everything changed. I realized that I did have a lot of practical knowledge about operating systems, networks, user accounts, and how they all connected. I also realized that I was trying to apply solutions that had worked for me on other machines instead of truly troubleshooting the problem at hand. You are looking for a candidate that has already had this revelation. A tech that truly "gets it."

Also, the best technicians have an outgoing personality coupled with strong technical knowledge. They can work well with their colleagues. When you interview them, you can hold a conversation without it feeling forced or awkward. Even though it's a situation that can traditionally be tense for the interviewee, how they interact with you should provide a strong understanding of their personality. They understand the value of creating meaningful relationships, which allows them to connect with the end user personally. You are looking for an individual that will make your teachers feel at ease about their technical issues.

Finally, the potential hire should have a plan for their future career. Planning shows that the candidate is actively taking control of their future, even if that future does not involve working in your district for more than a few years.
Don't settle. Never settle on these decisions. A weak or rushed hiring decision can drag your department down for years. These individuals do exist, but you may need to wade through

a lot of duds before you find someone who fits well with your organization.

3
Building Your Team

You may be reading this thinking, "Yeah, this is great stuff, except I do not get to pick my team. I inherited this squad for better or for worse. What now?" The inability to choose your team is a reality that most of us will face quite often in our careers. You will have to use the folks you have been given to support your environment for the foreseeable future. (unless you are working for a newly formed startup or you have been given the go-ahead from your Superintendent to clean house)

Just like in poker, your goal is to build the best hand with the cards you have been dealt. Your team, regardless of size, will most likely follow a bell curve. You will have some people who are a tremendous asset to your organization, while others are average at best. Some, though, are far worse than the rest. They may be the living embodiment of the word "struggle." So how do you make your best hand when some of your cards appear to be worthless? Upgrade or discharge those that are undesirable.

Everyone has room for professional growth, such as lack of attention to detail or low follow through on projects. These areas have been the subject of numerous self-help and improvement books. I want to focus on some specific personnel troubles typical in the information technology field, specifically in the K-12 sector.

Laziness

In my humble opinion, this is the most common technician related complaint in this industry. The reason I believe it's so prevalent is the age-old argument of perception versus reality. Is the employee truly lazy, or is that simply the public perception due to a lack of technical understanding? There are only two people that can answer that question: the employee and his immediate supervisor.

Regardless of the answer, addressing this issue should be a top priority. Laziness, actual or perceived, can spread like cancer through your department or organization. Let's follow this scenario a bit to understand better how laziness can create a nightmare.

Somebody has concluded that a member of the technology team is plain lazy. That individual mentions this observation to a coworker or two. The gossipers are going to gossip. Someone is bound to say something like:

> "Andy sits behind that computer and rarely leaves his desk. Honestly, I don't know what he does all day."

That comment generates some additional chatter, all suggesting that Andy is a lackluster employee. When one of those people needs help, they pick up the phone and call anyone but Andy because he is lazy and probably will not help them. The technician they call resolves their issue and reinforces the laziness perception by merely doing their job. It's a vicious cycle that triggers an even larger disaster.

Andy's teammates begin to hear that most people think he is lazy. Since his phone is not ringing much (because no one is calling him), those peers start to believe or even fuel the rumors. Now they have to pick up the slack for lazy Andy. Since his manager isn't addressing Andy's performance, this type of behavior is seen as acceptable, leading to a lack of respect for the supervisor. Peers may even begin to imitate it, knowing there are no real consequences.

The most effective way to handle a lazy employee is to have an open, direct conversation with that individual. Your first objective is to determine whether this is actual or perceived laziness. You probably have a good idea going into the conversation, but it is essential to keep an open mind. Before the meeting, collect a few examples of where it appears the person in question has not performed efficiently. Present your evidence in a "help me understand" format while ensuring to address the issue directly.

> Ex. "When rolling out those new desktop machines last week, you only set up fifteen while others managed to do thirty or thirty-five. Help me understand what prevented you from turning in similar numbers.

The response almost always acknowledges the mistake in perceived laziness and provides a legitimate reason, coupled with an apology. The individual knows they did not keep pace but can justify their performance issue.

> "Yeah, sorry about that. I was interrupted by a pressing issue in payroll, which took quite a bit of time to resolve. I should have touched base with you before heading over there."

On the other hand, actual laziness replies are often loaded with excuses to explain poor behavior.
- I wasn't feeling so well that day.
- Rodney was supposed to be helping me, but he didn't.
- I had to do all the ones on the 3rd floor, so of course, it's going to take me longer.

The determination you make relative to perceived or actual laziness should guide the rest of the conversation. What about those times when it is merely a problem with a gossiper, not the employee or even perception?". While that can be the case, taking a closer look at the situation can quickly help you decipher what is going on.

Precise communication with the offender is an excellent way to combat the perception of laziness. Start by explaining to the individual what the understanding about their performance is at the time. Be direct, but not harsh. We are talking about a reliable employee who does not always make the best choices regarding communication or efficiency. Use the time to talk about specific strategies that will help to change the perception. Additionally, in a perceived laziness scenario, use team meeting time to highlight what everyone is working on, stressing the "lazy" person's efforts. It shows the team that you and the individual in question are aware of the perception and are working to correct it.

CTOs should address actual laziness similarly. Be honest and direct. Let the person know that they are not pulling their weight on the team. Provide several examples of when you have witnessed the undesired behavior. If possible, use data from the work order system or other metrics with hard numbers. It's hard to dispute data. Explain your view on their productivity and then back it up with facts. These two points are vital aspects of the conversation.

Now that you've presented your views, give the team member time to respond. It is essential to listen to the response carefully. For them to grow professionally, they need to recognize that they have a problem. Without that realization, the behavior won't change. Over the years, I have worked with quite a few lazy people. The catch is that they did not consider themselves lazy. In their mind, they were putting in an honest day's work. A conversation like this one, where you are accusing someone of being lazy, may come as a total surprise, so it is essential to give them a chance to process and discuss before moving the conversation forward.

Once you have established that there is a problem, you can now work toward a resolution. Just like with perceived laziness, determine several specific strategies to change this behavior. For example, there's a ticket requesting a software package that will take 20 minutes to install. The setup process that requires technician interaction takes only a minute or so. Often, a tech will start the installation and then browse the web on their phone. Instead of wasting time waiting for the process to finish, they should be looking to make the most out of that time. Could they walk down the hall and swap a toner cartridge in the teacher's lounge? What about taking a few minutes to look at the weird software issue in the fourth-grade hall? As a leader, model this behavior when possible and "poke" your techs when they appear to be idle.

Ask them two simple questions:
- What else could you do while you wait?
- Is there a faster way you could do this install in the future?

Promote a culture that does not tolerate laziness by modeling productive behavior and publicly acknowledging decisive actions.

Bedside Manner
A second common issue with technical support staff is a rude or unprofessional attitude when dealing with teachers, especially those that are not tech-savvy. That attitude is a combination of arrogance coupled with a lack of patience. They act as if helping a person is a major inconvenience. If you have ever seen the Saturday Night Live skit with Jimmy Fallon as "Nick Burns: Computer Guy," you know exactly what I mean.

This type of behavior is unacceptable in any environment. In Educational Technology, though, a service industry by definition, it is even less acceptable. I have heard horror stories of technicians treating people so disrespectfully that the staff member has been brought to tears. You need to deal with behaviors like this swiftly. You cannot build a high performing, well-respected department with customer service individuals like this.

Similar to laziness, the best approach to this problem is a direct one. Schedule a meeting with the employee to discuss their attitude. Before the meeting, follow your district's procedure to document the conversation you are about to have with the individual. In my opinion, it's a good idea to do this before the meeting occurs. Documentation can easily get lost in the shuffle if you wait until afterward to write it up. Your frustration level drops after getting things off your chest, and you are less likely to set aside time to do the paperwork.

When the time comes to meet, start the conversation off by explaining the issue at hand. Be sure to include potential consequences if you do not see a change. Remember to maintain good eye contact when you speak.

> Example: "Jim, I've received several complaints about your negative attitude. I've witnessed it myself. I want to give you the opportunity to change your behavior based on the feedback I am about to provide before we need to reconsider your continued employment with the district."

Move the conversation forward by providing examples of where their actions, words, or tone were unprofessional. Take a moment to talk through each sample and to identify how they should behave in the future. Before moving on to another instance, ask them if they are clear on the issue and the plan of action going forward.

The final step in the process is to provide the employee with the documentation you completed earlier. Ask them to sign and date it, make a copy, and give that to the individual for their records. I suggest saving your document in an electronic format, ideally in the cloud. Documentation is a crucial piece to have if the behavior does not change. It will be the evidence showing you have addressed this concern with the employee in the past. We will touch more on this in a few pages.

Not on the same team

As we look at common personnel issues in education IT departments, we will end on the one that is much harder to resolve than the other two. Consider this scenario: You have a talented individual on your team. He has been in the district for a few years now, so he knows the infrastructure and end-user devices quite well. He is not lazy, nor does he have a bad report with the teachers. It sounds like just the kind of person you want on your side, right? Well, that is just it. He is not on your side.

He was passed over for your position and has a strong sense of entitlement. He holds it against you. Or he has an entirely different philosophy than you do regarding what technology is best and how the department should implement it. While he maintains a model persona for everyone else, he is an internal nightmare for you. He is always arguing with you, sometimes aggressively, sometimes passively. He is quietly rooting for you to fail, even helping it along by dragging his feet on high profile projects. It is causing a divide among the rest of the department, causing individuals to take sides.

This issue is difficult to resolve because you are not attempting to change a specific behavior. You are embarking on an endeavor to change someone's beliefs. Change is possible, but it is not easy. Focus on attempting to adjust their personal feelings related to the work environment you both share.

In my experience, the most effective way to address this is to start by having an open conversation about the apparent disagreements between you. Listening and discussing the topics at hand will lead to some resolution. End the conversation by reminding the employee that regardless of how you earned your position, you need to lead the district in the way you see fit. Lay out your vision for what technology looks like in the next few years. Clearly explain that while he will be given the opportunity to speak his mind along the way, you expect him to support the decisions that you make in the future.

The next step is to begin implementing your strategy and then use the results to add credibility to your design. In other words, do what you set out to do and let the result prove you know what you are doing. After some success in your new role, the divide on your team will begin to close. The change will not happen overnight. The road will be rocky at times. You may not change their beliefs, but you will earn the respect of your doubters. The key is staying the course and the success in the ultimate realization of your plan.

Motivate Them
We've taken the time to look at three common personnel issues you may face as a leader in Information Technology. The truth is you could see those traits in any organization, not just IT and not just within education. The issues we looked at should only affect a portion of your team. So what about the individuals in your department that are doing what they should be doing? How do you ensure they continue to be positive contributors?

All of us are motivated to succeed at some level. There is something that drives our need for success. For some people, that motivation is money. For others, it is public recognition of their efforts. I recommend individually meeting with each person on your team to understand their goals better and motivate them to reach those goals. You should consider doing this once each school year, maybe more if the situation warrants it. Keep a written account of what you discuss. When you meet again, the previous conversation can guide the interaction.

I've seen an incredible amount of value in this in my professional career. As a consultant, the organization's vice president asked to meet with me to discuss my future. He clearly articulated the purpose of the meeting before the sit-down, which served two purposes. First, it took the fear of the unknown out of the equation. I knew I was not walking into a termination meeting. Secondly, those meetings caused me to take a step back and focus on what motivated me, what I wanted to be, and how I wanted to get there. It helped to keep the fire burning and even encouraged me to push myself harder.

Documentation
Try as you might to address these common issues; some people refuse to change their ways. To quote a good friend of mine, "Their talents may be better used at another organization." Ending someone's employment is a harsh conclusion to reach, but it is not fair to you, your team, or the district to allow unwanted behaviors to continue. Going back to the poker example, you will need a strategy to discard the unusable cards in your hand.

The termination and reduction in force (RIF) guidelines differ for every district, but all of them require documentation that supports your recommendation for termination. You need to establish a pattern of unacceptable behavior, show evidence that you have addressed the issue with the individual, and provide examples of continued problems. Establishing a pattern cannot be completed overnight or even in a few weeks. It is a long, daunting process. I have spoken to numerous directors who have a bad apple on their team but refuse to take the necessary steps to terminate because of the effort involved.

When you have finally had enough, here are the keys to collecting the data you need.

Evaluations
Every employee is typically evaluated at least once per school year, although the process for evaluations is district specific. Use this opportunity to address the improper behavior with the individual. Complete the evaluation rubric assigning accurate point values and write out your concerns in the comments section. Review the evaluation with the employee in detail. Give specific examples that validate your concerns. Once you have finished going over the review, discuss measurable goals

to address the concerns you outlined. Set a deadline to revisit the goals you have established. Ask them to sign and date the document acknowledging that they understand your concerns and the established goals. As the supervisor, you should sign it as well. Provide them with a copy that includes both your signatures.

When you are creating goals, be sure that the description is written clearly with defined deliverables.

> Ex. Jason will send a summary of his work-related activities to his immediate supervisor by the end of the workday every Friday. The summary will include tickets he completed and an update on any outstanding projects he is a part of.

The reason for this is accountability. At the predetermined interval you established during the goal creation process, you can refer back to the defined objectives. It should be straightforward to verify if the goals have been accomplished. If Jason has not been sending a weekly report or has not been including the required information, he has not met the goal. If this pattern persists, you have the documentation needed to have a more substantial conversation with Jason about his future with the district.

Workspace Design

Anyone in the Information Technology field knows the power of teamwork. As you are reading this, think of a time when you called a colleague for help on a complicated issue. After exhausting most of your thinking, you reached out for the advice of someone who may have dealt with a similar problem in the past. Regardless of your position in the group (administrator, engineer, helpdesk, etc.), you rely on others' experience to help you solve challenging problems. There is a high likelihood that someone within your district or personal network will have experience in whatever issue you are facing in the edtech industry. There is probably an individual that has encountered a similar problem in the past.

Review this common scenario in a medium sized technology department made up of ten techs that support a large school district. The technicians are spread out across several buildings and typically focus on their assigned school or schools. John is a smart, hardworking technician who strives to get the most done during his workday as possible. As the days go on, John is consistently closing more tickets than everyone else by mapping out his day ahead of time and multitasking when possible. He will start imaging two machines and running updates on a third before he begins to tackle a laptop with a known virus problem. His superiors praise his efforts, and those users in his area speak highly of his skills. While this is fantastic for John and those he works with, he is mostly working in isolation. One-tenth of the district is very happy with their support, while the rest of the schools receive mediocre service. A successful team is one that shares a common space in a central location to the organization. My ideal setup for a technology team is a large, open area that houses everyone. Every team member should have their own desk and workspace, but cubicle walls or other barriers should not separate it. Every member of the team should be able to see and hear everyone else. My days as a consultant validated my theory of this type of environment time and time again. First and foremost, the open environment brings a sense of accountability to the team. I've been asked, "What does so-n-so actually do all day?" more times than I care to remember. With this model, everyone understands what their colleagues are working on because they can physically see them doing the work. This accountability can combat laziness or poor behavior while breeding efficiency. Imagine the same scenario only instead of a decentralized design, all of the technicians worked out of one location, and no one was assigned a particular area or department. The entire team sees John's highly efficient methods in action. They begin to question and evaluate his style themselves.

- How is he closing so many more tickets than I am?
- Why does the administration favor him?
- Why do users request John?

And most importantly...

- Do I want to be more like John?

The second advantage to the centralized approach is the collective knowledge that is assembled in one room. Each member of the team has taken a unique path to arrive in your district. They have seen distinctive setups, implemented different solutions, installed countless programs, and have access to their own unique experiences. The best part about that specific knowledge is that it is available to any team member with nothing more than a shout. "Hey, has anyone ever encountered this before?" Harness that remarkable knowledge base!

Often, when I am designing a strategy or kicking ideas around in my head, I will attempt to involve the whole room in the conversation by merely talking out loud so that everyone can hear my thoughts. I am sure my sudden stream of contemplations was initially unexpected, but as my colleagues got to know me, these open conversations became commonplace. When we would implement an idea that was so openly discussed in our office, everyone was on board and understood what to do. The buy-in was present through the collaborative creative process.

The reliance on peers creates a strong team mentality that is essential to the success of your department. Everyone needs to contribute to and be a part of the team. Every member must buy into the district's strategic vision. More importantly, the department's goals should align with and support that vision. Your group can suffer dramatically with a single outlier. Those who are not on board can destroy what everyone else is working to create due to a poor attitude. Using a model in which everyone works out of the same open area will strengthen your team, promote efficiency, and increase your department's overall knowledge.

Scheduling Your Techs

When I help a user, they often toss out one of my least favorite technology staffing ideas. They have thrown out what they believe is a game-changing suggestion, but it is a failure waiting to happen to me.

Let's create a weekly schedule of when a technician will be in the building so our people know when they can expect to receive help. A scheduled technician plan (STP)! We can work with the IT department and building leaders to develop an acceptable calendar and then disseminate that to our staff. If the building on the schedule for a time slot does not have any tickets, the technician can check in with the building leader. When the building leader confirms there are no outstanding issues, the tech can move on to a building with open work orders.

I have worked in this model as a technician and reluctantly implemented it for a few clients who were passionate about the idea. At first, the design may sound like a good one. Admittedly, the first time I heard it from our department head, I believed it to be a concrete suggestion as well. It took around six weeks for this idea to crash and burn like a modern-day air disaster. The results were ultimately the same, regardless of the size of the district or the technician involved. Ticket times had gone up, user dissatisfaction had risen, and staff morale had gone down drastically. What happened? Why had such a novel idea gone belly up so quickly?

There are three significant issues with the scheduled technician plan. As you read about these flaws, I must remind you that these conclusions are not the result of a single failed attempt to organize technical support. As a consultant, I watched several variations of this plan implemented (against my advice), only to end up with the same dismal fate as before.

Flaw #1: That's Our Time

Once a set amount of time is blocked off on an electronic

calendar, buildings begin to think of that as "our time." The issue arises when there are no outstanding tickets for that location. The technician has two options. They can go to the building and sit in standby mode or request to move on to a building with open work orders. Waiting for work is an obvious waste of time. (There is a whole section on why a tech should not go looking for issues, so I will not even touch on that here.) Most technicians ask the building principal if they are aware of anything that needs to be addressed, and assuming nothing comes up, they move on.

After several weeks of low ticket volume, the technician is routinely requesting to move on to other projects. Leadership begins to get the impression that they are getting no support from the IT department. The technician continues to inform building leadership that there are no outstanding problems at their location. The perceived lack of tech concerns is where the problems can begin to occur. The logical response is to get some tickets into the system so the building can feel like they are getting the support they need. Users are pressed to put in work orders, and the system gets flooded with "busy work" tickets. The staff is requesting support for issues that were not important enough to report for several weeks. These new tickets are suddenly priority items mostly due to leadership's pressure to put in tickets.

The result is leadership feels dissatisfied due to the perception their building is being neglected. The end-user is unhappy because now they have unresolved technology issues. Technician morale declines while they have to address loads of "invented issues" that are typically time-consuming or a pain to resolve in general.

Flaw #2: We got THAT guy / I got THAT building
Every team member is valuable, but let's face it, some technicians are better than others. They are approachable, personable and address issues with an "everything will be alright" demeanor. The staff at the buildings or locations where the better technicians are assigned will be confident that their

technology problems will be solved quickly and competently. What about the other side of that coin? What about the location that gets the stereotypical introverted technician? You know the one. The tech that struggles when working with people is considered lazy or cannot solve problems as quickly as possible. How will that building feel when they hear about this new plan for technology support?

You can say the same thing about buildings as technicians. Some schools are more straightforward to support than others. Your staff member who gets placed at the "bad buildings" may become disgruntled over their placement.

I know what you are thinking. You have already solved this issue. The technicians will rotate between locations to feel like they are getting the same amount of support. Unfortunately, that kind of rotation will further complicate the situation. Communication breakdowns between technicians become common in these scenarios.

A great example is when one tech attempts to resolve an issue that another tech had already begun to address. Your team winds up spending too much time trying to solve a problem because the two technicians have not discussed the resolution strategy. Your end-users also begin to lose faith in your team's ability to solve problems because they heard conflicting stories on what needed to be done to fix the problem.

Flaw #3 – Emergencies, Big projects, Make up Time

The final flaw of the scheduled technician plan is a lack of flexibility. A successful technology department is nimble. It can adapt quickly to the virus outbreak at the building across town by sending a swarm of techs to clean it up. When teamwork is required, highly effective IT departments can address the crisis at hand as a group. The STP model makes collaborative efforts very cumbersome.

Let's look at the virus outbreak example to understand this flaw better. It is Tuesday morning, and a virus has infected fifty machines, mostly in the administrative offices of several schools. The district is almost at a standstill. It is preventing the office staff from working, resulting in a disruption of the educational process. It needs immediate attention. You rally the troops and send your whole team to clean this nasty infection and get the organization back up and running. By the end of the day, your crew has scrubbed the infection clean from all of the machines. Success...right?

In banding together to help one location, your technicians had to abandon the usual Tuesday schedule. The following day, the team goes ahead with a regular Wednesday schedule. All of the users expecting to see their tech on Tuesday are frustrated because now they have to wait for their turn in the rotation again. You could try to prevent this by adjusting the schedule to avoid the virus building for the rest of the week while your team tries to catch up and visit the buildings they missed on Tuesday. The catch here is that the building with the virus problems had tickets in the system before the outbreak. Your team may have spent an entire day at that location, but they did not solve any of the outstanding issues because they were disinfecting computers.

The first time or two that a disaster occurs, people tend to understand it was an emergency. In that case, the needs of the few outweigh the needs of the many. They understand, but trust me; they do not forget. As time goes on, your team's ability to handle emergencies, device rollouts, lab imaging, and other big projects without disrupting the technician schedule will become impossible.

Conclusion
In the end, a successful scheduled technician plan is nothing more than a mirage in the desert of technical support. It looks like an oasis or a sanctuary from a distance. Once you make the long, arduous trip across the hot desert sand, you realize you have been tricked. It is not a sanctuary. It is a den of frustrated end users, angry administrators, and downtrodden

technicians.

Daily Plan & MITs

Productivity is never an accident. It is always the result of a commitment to excellence, intelligent planning, and focused effort. – Paul J. Meyer

Before stepping your foot in the door, you should have already crafted a plan for the day regardless of your position in the organization. In most cases, you should communicate that plan to your entire team the night before. Technicians should have a plan. Engineers should have a plan. Administrators should have a plan. Everyone on the team needs to be prepared for the day ahead before that day even begins. Take a minute to think about how your day starts. When you arrive at work, what do you do? Do you know precisely what you want to get accomplished that day? If you don't, you are wasting time while you make that determination. Even if you are waiting for your supervisor to arrive and lay out the strategy for the next eight hours, you waste time. Aside from wasting time, creating a plan every morning usually means that the team has not given much thought to what needs to get accomplished. Lack of forward-thinking breeds mediocrity.

A well designed daily plan should include three main areas:
1. Designate a certain number of jobs that must be completed that day. I refer to them as the Most Important Tasks (MIT). MITs is not my original concept, but it is one I use regularly. The number of tasks should depend on the team's size, but a quick calculation is 1.5 jobs for every person involved. These MITs should take precedence above everything else. These items will have a considerable positive effect on your department or prevent a significant negative impact. A great example of a most important task (MIT) is installing a software application in a lab full of computers. The install will positively impact everyone who plans to use

that lab. It also prevents the negative effect of someone sending a complaining email to the "higher-ups" about how they could not use the lab because IT had yet to install the software. Every MIT does not have to be an extensive, time-consuming project. It is merely taking the time to identify the high profile items and ensuring they get accomplished quickly.

2. The daily plan should include a combination of both tickets and projects. Often, IT departments focus on getting the number of tickets to a manageable number, all the while pushing projects off until things slow down. The problem is that ignoring large, time-consuming projects to tackle day-to-day issues can quickly lead to discontent among users. Imagine that you have been waiting for two weeks for the cable company to come out and move your satellite dish so that you will get better reception. During the two weeks since you asked for assistance, you see numerous cable technicians in your neighborhood taking care of small issues for your neighbors who put in tickets after you did. Can you see how this would be frustrating? Make sure your plan includes a blend of tickets and projects.

3. Finally, the daily schedule needs to be flexible. The world of information technology support can be flipped upside down with a single failed hard drive, a virus-laden link, or some other catastrophe that becomes the fire of the day. You need to account for the unknown issues that may cause a ten-minute task on the schedule to take forty-five minutes. In other words, do not try to cram too many jobs into each day.

Taking the time to create and communicate a plan before starting the workday that incorporates the three points listed above will help ensure your team is a productive one.

Weekly Meeting
Meetings are a necessary evil. I can accomplish quite a bit in

a meeting with a purpose and an agenda. Some of the best ideas come from discussions with a group of colleagues that are genuinely engaged in a conversation.

Every week, the entire department should meet as a group. My preference is to have these meetings on Monday morning around 8:30 am. An agenda should be given to the team on Friday afternoon to allow your staff to prepare for Monday. The discussion should have four primary goals. Barring any significant announcements, each part should only take about 5-10 minutes. While the meeting is taking place, one person should be taking notes, paying particular attention to any additional duties assigned during the session.

When the meeting has concluded, ask the person who took the notes to email each person with any assigned tasks. It is not uncommon that someone will agree to take on a particular responsibility, only to forget that commitment five minutes after leaving the meeting. I believe this strategy of emailing each individual dramatically increases the chances of the task getting completed.

- **Strategy Review** – This is a simple reminder of what your team is trying to accomplish this week. While it may seem like overkill, you drive the point home that the current strategy is essential. The team should take the strategy review seriously.

  For example, the month of September's goal is to decrease the number of open tickets to somewhere below twenty. During the weekly meeting, address the progress toward the target and provide some encouragement".

  Our team managed to close sixty-five tickets last week. We only had thirty-one new tickets hit the work order system, so we had a net gain of thirty-four. That's an impressive accomplishment, team! Keep it up. Remember, we are trying to get below twenty before the month is over to focus our attention on the wireless upgrade in October. "

- **Project Review** - Typically, in IT, multiple projects are happening simultaneously in addition to keeping up with the day to day tickets. Use ten minutes of the meeting, asking those involved to share the projects' status, making sure to include any obstacles or successes that occurred. Even if you are aware of the situation, have the team review the progress for all to hear to ensure that everyone is on the same page.

"Jen, can you please give us an update on where we are with the new voicemail system? The notes from last week stated we were waiting on AT&T to resolve a DID issue. "

- **Follow Ups** – Use this time to verify that team members accomplished tasks assigned to them in last week's meeting. Completing the job itself is essential; the accountability of the designated individual should be equally as important. If you believe the assignment should have been taken care of, do not be afraid to let them know you are disappointed. Do it in private, though. It does need to be addressed; however, public reprimand or embarrassment is rarely effective. After the meeting, speak with the person to discuss why the project did not get finished and what steps can be taken to resolve the issue.

- New Business – Lastly, take some time to discuss any upcoming decisions, projects, or plans. I prefer to save this until the end of the meeting. Items in the category are usually positive, and I believe it helps end the session positively.

Get Social
Social media, specifically sites like Twitter and Instagram, are changing the way we get our information. As a director of

technology, that is an indisputable fact of life for me. I ignored Twitter for the first nine years after it hit the scene. I barely kept up on Facebook and LinkedIn. The thought of adding another social network to my plate was daunting. In my eyes, it was another distraction in an already busy life. Besides, what did it have to offer that I couldn't just get from CNN or the Huffington Post?

I could not have been more wrong. The best analogy is to think of Twitter as a large party or gathering of people, all having conversations about different topics. At first glance, there are so many conversations going on that it seems like an endless stream of random information. Just like a party, though you are not a part of every conversation. You are active in those conversations that interest you. When you navigate the site to find the subjects and topics that matter to you, some amazing things can happen.

Here are three examples of the great tweets that have led to very positive outcomes.

- After seeing a tweet on 21st-century activities for teachers, we started a contest within our district that revolved around that post. It has brought a whole new level of engagement to our staff and students.
- A tweet regarding upcoming awards for digital innovators pushed us to nominate several staff members. While we didn't win any awards, it provided a way to highlight some of the awesome things our teachers are doing.
- A Google executive and professional role model of mine tweeted about an upcoming trip to Northeast Ohio. After a few tweets and some emails, he agreed to speak to our teaching staff to discuss how technology is changing education.

While those examples are exceptional in their way, they may not apply to your industry or organization. This book is supposed to help you build confidence in your technical team. Let's take a minute to look at some practical ways you can use social media, specifically Twitter, to make a real impact on your organization.

Social Techs

By now, it should be clear that technical knowledge is not the only factor that makes a great technician. The best technicians have an outgoing personality coupled with strong technical knowledge. Twitter is a perfect outlet to showcase their personality. I encourage technicians to tweet a balanced mix of technical "geek stuff," coupled with aspects about their lives outside of work. This mix of work and personal tweets helps create a stronger bond between them and the district stakeholders. It is similar to a modern version of "water cooler" chats, but these chats occur in cyberspace.

Here is a real-world example of the type of Twitter exchange I am referencing. With just a single tweet, the tech made a personal connection with the staff member.

> @Tech: We're playing like all-stars on defense; let's keep this up! #Browns
> Staff Member Reply: @Tech Liking this side of you! Go Brownies!!

Let's look at some of the ways techs can use social media in your department.

Information Decimation

There's a need to get information out to every employee and stakeholder in a timely fashion. Social media sites like Twitter, Instagram, and, to some extent, Facebook can be the fastest way to get important information out quickly. As I stated before, social media is changing the way people get their information. Stop and think about that statement for a minute. Where do breaking news stories typically get their start? Someone has sent a tweet and attached a picture of what they saw. Credible news outlets then investigate and report further, vetted information.

In my opinion, it is no longer acceptable to only post information to the web or send out a mass email. Embrace this change! Use your Twitter account to send out alerts of a planned or unplanned network outage, promote a new system you have implemented, or provide a quick tip to your employees.

Recognition

Social media is an incredible platform for publicly recognizing deserving people, successful projects, and unique innovations. A terrific example of public recognition occurred just a few months ago. I firmly believe that talented desktop support technicians are the unsung heroes of educational IT. These folks spend their days helping others but are rarely given the appreciation they deserve. To change that, a few of us organized a campaign to thank Steve, the technician in our district, publically. It started by sending a mass email to the faculty and staff in the district that use Twitter. The email explained that on Dec 17th, please take a moment to say "Thank You" on Twitter, making sure to end the message with #SteveRocks.

The results were terrific! Steve received over fifty direct tweets along with countless favorites and retweets. Those tweets reached an audience of thousands of people. He was shocked by the outpouring of gratitude. With just an idea and an email, we could publicly recognize someone for all of their hard work and show our appreciation. When people talk about the power of social media, this is what they mean.

Connections

Social media provides direct access to people that would otherwise be out of reach. Using sites like LinkedIn and Twitter, I've made connections with industry experts, thought leaders, and IT directors across the country. I can reach out to those individuals when the need arises. Those same people occasionally ask for my input as well. It is not just a one-way street. That is the incredible side to all of this.

With Information dissemination and public recognition, the amount of work you need to invest is minimal. To have a network of connections on social media, you have to build your network first. The process is not complicated, but it is laborious at first. There are some tremendous resources (sites, podcasts, books) out there on how to build your network. I would encourage you and your technicians to do the research and then make an effort to become an active contributor to social media. As you add value to these networks, others will notice, and good things will follow.

Make Them Read
Keeping apprised of new ideas and trends in technology is essential. It is vital to keep up to date to avoid falling into a technology rut in your day to day routine. Though it seems like common sense to stick with what works for your team, this is not always true. IT is an industry that is continually changing. Whether new hardware, software, or applications, each can offer your device innovation that could ultimately save time, money, and frustration. Though this may not be true for every update, the ones that provide advantages are well worth knowing about as early as possible.

As the district IT department, your team is perceived as the local experts in all subjects related to technology. You know you will get asked about the latest or newest updates, apps, and hardware. People will want to see what you think about that new Apple device or the cool gadget someone heard about at a conference. You need to have an answer and not just a generic one. You need to add fuel to the fire that will keep up the perception that you are indeed an expert. If teachers and district administrators cannot rely on you for up to date technology details, they will turn elsewhere. Is that what you want? The folks who depend on you are now asking their neighbor's cousin, who helps fix the computers at his church, for specifics on the new iPhone and its potential uses in the classroom.

Reading about what others are doing with technology can be

a tremendous source of inspiration. Think about how many times you have heard about someone else's innovative concept. I can't be the only one who immediately attempts to adapt their idea or design to fit your needs. In my opinion, stories like this cause you to look at your model from a different perspective. A new point of view can open the flow of creativity.

The best way to avoid becoming stagnant or out of touch is to set time aside each week to keep current. I typically dedicate an hour each week to reading blogs and reviewing sites related to educational technology. Sites such as Edudemic, Tech & Learning, LifeHacker, and CNet are personal favorites. Typically, I will check these sites every few days. Twitter is also a great place to find out what other conversations are happening. Log on to the site and search for tags like #edtechchat and #edtech. As you scroll through the tweets, you will begin to see what websites are popular among teachers and integrationists worldwide. In addition to reading, sometimes, I will listen to podcasts during my daily commute. Shows like This Week in Tech (TWIT), Tech Meme Ride Home, and The TED Radio hour are informative and motivating at the same time.

Encourage your team to do the same by providing time each week for reading about technology. Carving out time for your team will serve a dual purpose. It helps to keep team members up to date and may improve their writing and communication skills. If you model and stress this type of behavior, both you and your team will benefit. Many years ago, I had a boss who would scan interesting articles to leave on my desk. Though it was not something I understood or appreciated at the time, it is a habit I now have with my team. Staying current is a precious tool.

Make Them Write
The ability to communicate ideas, instructions, and thoughts in a clear, well-composed manner is an essential aspect of the IT industry, though it is often overlooked. Everyone in an IT

department should be able to communicate well in person and in their writing. Just as with other skills, this is accomplished best through practice. Writing may take on a variety of forms but should meet the criteria outlined below.

The world at large preaches "practice makes perfect." The same notion applies here. This adage can be used to the communication skills of an IT department. This does not mean that you should ask your team to write a single document, but they should practice the skill as often as possible. Your department's size and structure, coupled with the type of writing needed (blogs, how-tos, product reviews), will play a large role in what defines "often" for your group. In my experience, writing three paragraphs every two weeks is an excellent starting point. Adding writing to your team's responsibilities is often an idea that is not well received, so expect resistance. The most challenging aspect is the writer not knowing what to write about, how long this should be, or how often it is expected. Clarify these aspects in the beginning to encourage cooperation, including assigning topics. We will touch on choosing topics shortly, but let's look at the second component of developing well-written communication.

The second criterion in helping a writer progress over time is to make the writing available for public consumption, regardless of form. Posting their work online adds accountability for what is written and assures a certain level of quality control. Would you want colleagues, peers, and strangers to read your work if you knew it was not well written or contained simple proofreading errors? When you create something you are proud of, you want to share it with anyone who will read it. A real confidence boost can be felt when a colleague, friend, or teacher shares how much the article you wrote.

One way to bring the different writing styles and content together is through the creation of a website. Task each department member with creating content specific to their area of interest in technology. For example, some might choose to write about technology trends while others might gravitate toward sharing their experiences with new products. Create a schedule of individual due dates for everyone to ensure fresh content is published to the site every week or so. Utilize social media to direct people to your site. Email the entire district with the link to this great new resource the IT department has created. If your department is too small to maintain something like a website, consider asking team members to compose a weekly email to the staff with a helpful tip or review. A monthly newsletter also works well for smaller departments.

This model is a fantastic method to build your team's written communication skills and boost their confidence. When done correctly, the result is a tremendous asset to the rest of the company. It is a true win-win for everyone.

Make Them Speak

In the last section, I focused on the importance of strong written communication skills. However, the written word is just one aspect of a well-rounded communicator. The ability to speak in front of a room full of people is not something that comes easily to most, but it can be developed with practice like anything.

Professional development days are an excellent time for your technicians to practice speaking to an audience. Twice a year, ask each team member to lead a professional development session on a topic that they feel would be useful to the staff. Since these days do not typically involve staff members from other districts, your techs should feel a bit more comfortable than if they were presenting to a group of complete strangers. Additionally, allowing them to choose the subject will take some of the pressure off the presentation. You will want to review the topic before inviting staff members to attend to assess the speaker's appropriateness and preparedness.

As a leader, your goal is to help team members refine their

public speaking presence while simultaneously building confidence. In the first few minutes of the presentation, make eye contact, and provide a little gesture, like a head nod or thumbs up, to encourage the speaker and let them know things are going well. As the session continues, please pay close attention to what is being said, but avoid interrupting unless you are called upon or it is necessary. It can be difficult to stay silent, but speaking up to correct a mistake can quickly derail the session. Public correction can be humiliating and disheartening. If correct is needed, do so in private during a break so the presenter can correct the error during the session or upon completion of the session.

Members of the tech department who are not presenting should be expected to attend the sessions given by their peers. This allows those not presenting to create their own presentation based on what worked and what did not for fellow team members. This also allows your team members to see how an administrator or leader should behave during a presentation. Remember to be attentive, but for the most part, quiet.

When the session is over, participants should be prepared to provide constructive feedback to the presenter. This feedback does not need to be too in-depth or critical, especially for those who do not have much experience presenting to groups. Presenters should expect these feedback sessions and prepare ahead of time to answer potential questions and concerns. There are real growth opportunities when colleagues provide productive criticism.

In my experience, the best professional development sessions:
- Are not overly technical for the audience
- Are more than just examples or demonstrations. If the goal is to show the group how they can use Google Forms to replace a traditional pen and paper quiz, ask them to bring a paper quiz they use in their classes to the session so they can work on it while learning the program

- Interact with the audience or allow the audience to follow along on their own device.
- Include time for participants to create content based on what they have learned

4
Internal & External Support

Technology Advocates
Designing technology initiatives for teachers can be challenging for someone who has never actually been a teacher. You have probably led various professional development sessions with your staff, but that's nothing compared to a classroom full of twenty-five ten year olds. One of the most notable aspects of a highly effective IT department is a strong connection to the classroom. The initiatives you want to implement may look great on paper, but how can you be sure they will be successful in the teacher's hands? It would be best if you had a sounding board; a group of teachers you can bounce ideas off will give you honest comments and criticisms. It would help if you had people who trust that the department values their input and will adjust plans accordingly, based on the feedback provided.

The most effective way I have been able to establish those trust and create open communication lines is by selecting a "Technology Advocate" in each building. It is crucial that each building have representation in this group. It is a good idea to include the head of the librarians and media specialists in this group as well. Selecting a technology advocate should be a joint effort between you and the building principal, as there may be some cultural considerations to consider. Depending on your district's size, you may find value in choosing multiple tech advocates for your more substantial buildings.

So what makes a good tech advocate? An effective technology advocate possesses strong communication skills and has the respect of his or her colleagues. The technology advocate needs to communicate with both the Office of Technology & Information Systems and their colleagues about various technology projects and plans. The building technology advocate will facilitate communication between your department and the staff at his or her building. A technology advocate does not need to be the most tech-savvy person in the building, but a good understanding of technology is vital for success in the position. I consider this critical to success because the technology advocate becomes the de facto "go to" person in the building for simple technical issues.

For example, when someone cannot print, they ask their tech advocate for help before submitting a ticket. The tech advocate's class time and planning periods may be interrupted from time to time. There will be days when they come in early or leave late because they are helping a colleague troubleshoot a problem. They may get text messages during dinner, asking if the grade book application is down. To a certain degree, a tech advocate becomes a level one technician. It is because of this that I recommend that this position be a paid supplemental contract. Without compensation, it gives off the impression that you do not respect or value their time and that you are taking advantage of them. I have helped many districts implement the tech advocate model, and compensation played a significant factor in everyone's success or failure. Every single successful implementation provided payment.

How do I use them?
Once the group has been established, I suggest holding three ½ day meetings throughout the school year with required

attendance. I typically meet in October, February, and May. Use this time to discuss current and upcoming projects, brainstorm new ideas, and review technology issues specific to each building. When creating your meeting agenda, I recommend saving a portion of the meeting dedicated to reviewing technology issues until the end. There are three reasons for this decision:

- Keeps the attitude of the meeting positive.
- Prevents wasting time in a "bitch session."
- It is likely that you will touch on their issues during other parts of the agenda. You may answer their questions or concerns before they ever have a chance to ask them.

Outside of the meetings, make sure to keep the lines of communication open. Again, these are your eyes and ears at each building. When they hear colleagues speaking about technology concerns, you want tech advocates to feel comfortable informing you of those apprehensions. You can achieve this level of confidence by returning the favor. Use tact when contacting the staff member(s) that expressed concerns by not revealing who reached out to you.

> "Good Morning Dana
>
> I've heard that you might have some concerns with the new grade book package we are getting ready to introduce. I would love to hear your thoughts, ideas, and misgivings. Do you have some time to meet in the next week or go over those with me?
>
> Thanks
> Mike"

I typically BCC the tech advocate on a response like this. I want them to know that I took action on what they passed along. I also want that person to know I did not "tattle" on them.

Last, make an effort to take care of your tech advocates. Provide them a heads up when you know a project is going to impact their building or area. When they submit a work order, do your best to resolve it quickly. How can they be expected to fix other people's technology issues when they are experiencing problems of their own? Arrange for them to have access to try out new equipment. For example, if you see an innovative, lightweight, wireless document camera, purchase a few and give them to your tech advocates. They will appreciate the extra technology for their classroom and, in turn, will provide you with an honest review of how it works.

Technology advocates provide you with a window into the classroom. They can look at your upcoming initiatives from a unique perspective and provide direct feedback from the people that your decisions influence the most. Include them in your planning process, show them you value their opinions, and in return, they will become your voice to the staff. Their influence and enthusiasm will do amazing things for technology in their building, things you cannot do because you are not a classroom teacher.

Integrationist / Tech Coach

In my opinion, every single school district should have at least one technology integrationist on staff. An integrationist's role is to assist the teachers in overcoming the "hurdle of how." If you have spent any time in public education, you are probably very familiar with the "hurdle of how": "How can I use this in my classroom?". I believe the best technology integrationists are former teachers. It does not matter what subject, grade level, or school in which they taught. What matters is that they have experience in the classroom. The skillset and expertise they bring to the table is the key to their success. As a Director of Technology for a public school district, I have five reasons why an integrationist is vital to a district's technology implementation strategy:

1. They View Technology Differently Than You Do

A strong technology integrationist does not typically view technology in the same way we geeks do. Where we see an online photo editor, they see a creative outlet for students in social studies. We see a new web-based link organizer, while they see an app that would make an excellent tool for creating digital student portfolios. They have a way of looking at the web from an entirely different point of view. In my role, I seek out this viewpoint, especially when we are looking to adopt a new application or device. The collaboration that follows leads to a better understanding of what tools will work best for students and staff.

2. They Deliver Professional Development Better Than You Do

I pride myself on my ability to teach teachers. However, no matter how good you are at teaching others how to use technology, you cannot overlook experience in the classroom. Many integrationists genuinely understand the planning it takes to create a tech-based lesson and the frustration that occurs when that lesson does not go as planned. They embed that unique knowledge into their teaching, which allows them to connect with teachers on a level that most cannot.

3. They Can Be a Catalyst for Change

A technology integrationist can be an evangelist for your plans and ideas. Their enthusiasm for a new application, model, or design can be infectious. When they get excited about a newly discovered application, the staff listens. Why? The excitement comes from a trusted source who knows firsthand how they are using technology in the classroom. This is an often overlooked yet vital aspect of this role.

4. They Can Be Places When You Can't

A technology integrationist can spend time in the classroom daily, helping teachers at the point of instruction. You could too if it were not for your administrative meetings, tackling that wireless issue, investigating new potential solutions, and keeping up with the IT department's day-to-day activities. It can be challenging to make time for classroom visits. An integrationist can be your eyes and ears within the school. They can provide insights on what is working and what is not related to technology, which allows you to adjust strategies and policies accordingly. It is like having a window directly into the classroom.

5. **They Can Take Your District to the Next Level**
When you combine the reasons listed above with a strong technology department, the outcomes are phenomenal! We have seen an increase in staff engagement and technology use in and out of the classroom. Our teaching staff is trying new applications and ideas regularly. For example, we have staff using sites like Twitter and Instagram in their curriculum. They can do this because they feel supported in the use of digital tools across all content areas.

In my twenty years of working in educational IT, this is my first time working with a full-time integrationist dedicated to our district. This has easily been one of the best years of my career. Our teaching staff is using technology to enhance their curriculum in new ways, and our students are experiencing personalized learning thanks to her efforts. Every school district, every student, and every teacher needs to experience the positive impact that can be made by a thoughtful, enthusiastic, full-time technology integrationist.

Summary
A strong integrationist, especially one with a teaching background, can support your teachers in ways that a typical technology director cannot. For starters, their classroom experience allows them to see different solutions to a problem. They have various tools at their disposal that you may not be as familiar with. They can use those tools along with their teaching experience to deliver exceptional professional

development to your teachers. When problems arise, an integrationist can often drop everything to support a staff member who needs immediate assistance. Well designed professional development coupled with a flexible schedule and an intimate understanding of the classroom can take the district to a whole new level of technology engagement. As an IT leader, your job is to support the integrationist(s) with a reliable network, functional equipment, and fast work order resolutions so that teachers and students feel confident when using technology in their classroom.

External Support – Tech Committee
You are surrounded by industry specialists regardless of where your district is located. You have community members that go to work every day in careers that range from marketing to manufacturing, finance to production. A significant portion of these community members are parents that have students in attendance at your schools. Take a moment to contemplate the value of what I am saying. Within a few miles of your school district, you have access to experts in a comprehensive variety of subjects, many of whom have a vested interest in your success. This is an incredible resource that many organizations would pay substantial amounts of money to access. As a leader, you need to harness the collective power of this vast knowledge base that is available to you.

You can accomplish this by establishing a technology committee comprised of teachers, administrators, and district stakeholders. The process to create this group is a simple one. Start by inviting the technology advocates to join the committee. They will provide the connection directly back to the classroom that is crucial when making decisions about the future. Next, personally email each of the district administrators and building principals, asking them to participate in this new cohort. Explain that the committee will provide input on district initiatives related to technology and that the group will want to hear their ideas and concerns in these discussions. In the same email, ask them to identify two parents or community members they believe would be thoughtful contributors to the committee. After collecting their suggestions, send a similar email to those parents. Explain the committee's purpose, how they were selected, and articulate how their input as committee members is valuable to the planning process.

I recommend holding three ninety-minute meetings per year. Be sure to respect the committee member's time by wrapping up the session within that time. Your committee will become a dreaded activity quickly if members feel they will be trapped for hours on end.

First Meeting
You will want to wait until the chaos of a new school year has ended before a first meeting; mid-October typically allows for this to occur. The purpose of the first meeting should be two-fold in nature.

- Provide the group with a brief update on the work your team accomplished over the summer and the work that is planned for the next few months. The update should be no more than fifteen minutes. Try to avoid being overly technical during your update. No doubt there are highly complex initiatives to cover, but your audience does not want to hear about how you are painstakingly recreating your DHCP scopes.
- It would be best if you spend the remaining time brainstorming ideas for the following school year. You will need to start the dialogue by laying out the plans that are already in place. For example, if you know you are installing a new wireless network, let the group know that upfront. This way, you do not spend twenty minutes listening to stories of how bad the existing system is performing. From there, ask the group to offer up suggested projects or concerns they would like to see addressed. In a brainstorming session, try to keep the feeling in the room positive and comfortable. Do not squash an idea immediately, even if it seems off course or farfetched. As the meeting organizer, you can guide the conversation, but keep in mind that you invited everyone to hear their opinions, so let them speak. I like

to use a projector and laptop during this process to take notes on a Google Doc that everyone can see. Make sure to assign a note-taker so that it is added to the notes if an idea is thrown out there. The rest of the school year is spent refining the ideas and direction set forth by this meeting. You must engage the parents, community members, and teachers during this planning phase.

- With about fifteen minutes left, use your notes to summarize what the committee has discussed. Review these ideas to ensure you have accurately captured the key points raised. Finally, select a date for the next meeting and dismiss the committee. Make sure to thank everyone for coming and share your notes with the group. I usually try to share the notes before closing down my laptop for fear that I will forget to do it later.

Second Meeting
The second meeting should be held in late January or early February. You will have taken the time to research, analyze, and refine the ideas that came out of the initial meeting. At this meeting, you will present a draft of the project plan for the upcoming school year for the committee to review. When you send out the agenda for the meeting, be sure to include a short description of each initiative along with the estimated costs. This allows everyone the opportunity to review the document before the meeting. This second meeting aims to gather critical feedback from the committee members on the areas of the draft that do not meet their expectations. A few thoughts for this meeting include:
- Taking the time to explain each of the initiatives you have designed. If you had to change or even cut out some ideas altogether, inform the group of the logic behind those decisions.
- Encourage people to voice any concerns they may have. It is the last chance they will have to offer significant changes before you seek approval to move forward.

- Do not be discouraged if you are asked to go back to the drawing board with an idea or two. These folks have had months to think about what was discussed at the last meeting. They have probably talked to a few people and heard feedback on those ideas. There is a good chance they will want to incorporate the input and their thoughts into your design.

Final Meeting
As the school year comes to a close, it is a great time to have your final technology committee meeting. Over the last several months, you have taken the time to finalize the plan for the new school year. You will have spoken to the administrative team to determine what projects can be accomplished and which ones will need to be put back on the shelf. In this final meeting, I expect you to do most of the talking as you bring the technology committee back to the table to outline the strategy you have put together. Be sure to remind everyone how you arrived at the projects through discussions at the first two meetings. The initiatives themselves should not need too much explaining. You have merely tweaked them since the last meeting, but don't just skim through them either. Highlight the educational impact you expect to make. Finally, take this time to discuss the implementation timeline and address any potential roadblocks. When you are finished, thank the members for their contributions and answer any questions.

Rinse, Repeat
When the new school year begins, start all over with the first meeting and repeat the process. A note of caution: Once the group is confident in the direction the district is moving, attendance at the meetings may begin to dip. Consider inviting new members to join the committee each year to provide new perspectives. In my opinion, this cyclical meeting design offers a fantastic forum for district stakeholders to have a say in the future of technology in the schools.

External Support - Other Directors

IT directors in other school districts can be a tremendous source of both knowledge and inspiration. These are people who walk in your shoes every day. They have firsthand knowledge of the types of decisions you are asked to make. Having an open line of communication with at least a few of these folks is very beneficial. Chances are they are having similar conversations in their district about the same problems you have on your own. While they understand the issue at hand, they may have a different perspective on how to handle it. You can begin to trade thoughts and ideas on how to resolve a common problem with just a simple email or phone call.

The best part about this type of sharing is that you will not need to say or do much to initiate the conversation. The stereotype is that we IT geeks are introverts who do not like to talk, especially to someone outside our circle. That is so far from the truth. Most IT directors love to share their ideas with anyone who will listen. We are proud of the solutions we have designed! We want other IT people to hear about them. Think about your regional or state email listserv. Some individuals chime in on almost every single thread. Why? They spend their days solving problems. If the answer they came up with can help someone solve their problem, it is a bonus.

My advice would be to reach out to a few of the IT directors from area districts. Choose the people who tend to be vocal at meetings or whose name you have heard mentioned before. I would select five people and set up a time to meet with them individually. The meeting's goal is to better understand their school's technical makeup and the strategies used to manage it. Be upfront about your intentions. There is value in sharing, and you are looking for people with which to collaborate.

One question I like to ask when I do this is, "Would you share with me something you are doing that you are proud of?" Every technology person should have an answer for this. Usually, it is a new, creative mindset or way of thinking they implemented to solve a long-standing problem. This allows the person to brag a little about their accomplishments, which can be positive. This helps open the door to sharing ideas and builds trust between you and your new colleague. After the meeting, please make a point to check in with them on a semi-regular basis.

I bounce ideas off my IT friends almost weekly. They provide a great sounding board, as well as a critical eye. Discussing, or even arguing with them, results in a more polished solution. I enjoy hearing about their successes and their failures. Yes, I enjoy stories of where my friends have failed. It is not at all malicious or spiteful. In my opinion, failing forces you to be creative. I genuinely appreciate hearing about the issue, the miscues, and the thinking that leads to a successful outcome.

External Support – Engineers
Talented network engineers that truly understand public schools are difficult to find. What makes individuals like this so unique is their experience working within multiple school districts. Often, engineers will be asked to accomplish the same goal for several districts, but with different parameters and hardware at each site. These guys have not just heard about online testing but have helped numerous districts implement it on an assortment of devices. They can discuss the pros and cons of both bring your own device and 1:1 computing because they have had to design wireless networks to accommodate both of these models. You should feel incredibly fortunate if you are lucky enough to connect with someone like this. Their available knowledge base can be invaluable at times.

I developed a friendship with someone who fits the mold I described above during my days as a consultant. We worked on quite a few projects together over the years, and he always brought a unique perspective to the table. When working on a particularly challenging issue, I would lay out the potential solution to get his input. His networking expertise and unbiased opinion were always welcome. He was able to look at the design from both an infrastructure standpoint and an educational one.

We have both moved on to new positions with different organizations. We continue to speak weekly about challenges, philosophies, or concepts related to educational IT. Many books, podcasts, and blogs discuss the idea of surrounding yourself with people that "up your game." Having someone who can challenge your ideas and provide critical feedback can help you take your game to a whole new level. I would encourage you to seek out someone who can do the same for you.

Summary

The team of people you assemble to handle the school district's daily technical needs will always be a critical factor in your success. It is more significant than just individuals with strong technical skills. A highly successful IT department is more than just a fix-it shop with quick turnaround time. You need to build a team of people who understand that the IT department does not operate within a vacuum. These are people who will be active contributors to district conversations, using traditional means and social media to add value to that conversation. It is an organized group of technically skilled individuals working together to move a district forward.

A well-designed team works from a central location to utilize their collective knowledge base to resolve problems quicker and more efficiently. The whole group meets every week and focuses on student-centered, data-driven decisions. Daily plans are created and communicated to everyone to emphasize daily wins and promote transparency among the team. Collaboration occurs both internally with teachers and externally with resources, such as other directors or network engineers. The actual value is placed on the input from district stakeholders such as students, teachers, parents, and community members.
The team also shares a belief in the significance of reliable

customer service skills. As a leader, you have created an environment that encourages teachers to ask questions, even "stupid" ones. Technicians understand that technology does not come easily to everyone. They take pride in fixing an issue and explaining the problem in a way that the staff can understand. They take it a step further, providing sessions during professional days, after hours, or in some cases, on an individualized basis. They strive to provide the kind of customer service experience you would share with your friends.

At the end of the day, you can depend on a team of people to meet your needs. Every team member is willing to stay late, come in early, and do what it takes to make sure teachers and students are supported when using technology.

5
Ticketing Systems

Now that you have the right personnel for the job, you will want to focus your efforts on implementing a dynamic ticketing system for tracking, completing, and analyzing technical issues. The data that the system houses will guide your decision making and daily planning. Your technicians will spend a portion of their time every single day working within this system. End users inside your organization will use this as their primary avenue for support. Your ticketing system will be the backbone of your entire department. It is critical that you recognize the importance of this application before making a selection from the hundreds of options available. There are three aspects of a traditional ticketing system that must be considered:

· Public-facing / End-user side
· Technical side
· Administrative features

Public-Facing
Begin by examining the public-facing side of a well-designed ticketing system. Your work order application is what your teachers and support staff will use to tell your team about the

problems they are experiencing. Depending on the size of your district, this may very well be the only interaction those folks have with the IT department. Their interaction with your ticketing system must be a positive one. If it is difficult to report an issue, then frustration levels with technology can increase substantially and prevent use in the classroom. Decreased use in the classroom due to technical issues that last thing you want.

Keeping the end-user experience in mind, submitting tickets to the chosen system should be a straightforward process. The application needs to be cloud-based and accessible from anywhere, on any device with an internet connection. In this digital world, this concept should be a "no brainer." A system that is not cloud-based (or at least web-based) should not have a place in your organization.

Authentication Is a Must
Users should be required to log in, ideally authenticating with an existing system such as G Suite for Education or Active Directory. While it may seem more comfortable upfront to skip the authentication process, it is a disaster in the long run. Imagine this scenario:

The principal of West Elementary wants to know exactly how many tickets Mary Ann Johnson has submitted this year. She has been complaining about the lack of responsiveness of your team. The principal is aware that Mrs. Johnson likes to complain. The principal is questioning whether or not Mary Ann even entered the tickets. Instead of requiring users to authenticate, the system you chose asks them to submit their name with the ticket. When you go to look at the data, you see only three tickets for Mary Ann Johnson. You quickly report your findings to the principal, seemingly confirming her

findings. Two hours later, the principal is in your office, misinformed and very angry. She is armed with proof that Mary Ann had submitted fifteen work orders this year. Mrs, Johnson kept a copy of the email generated when the tickets were entered. As you dig into this more closely, you see that when she opened the tickets, she did not always use "Mary Ann Johnson." A few times, she used "Mrs. Johnson." In other cases, she used "Mary Johnson" or just "M A Johnson." You have provided inaccurate data to the building leader, and she has confronted an employee using that same inaccurate data. Guess who is in the dog house now?
Authenticating the user gives you an automatic tracking system for every ticket they submit. It does not rely on the end-user who can unknowingly provide inaccurate data. Authentication is a must.

Entering Tickets
Once a user is logged in, they should be presented with a form to open a new ticket. The form should already know who they are based on their login. There is no point in asking for a name if they are already logged into the system. The system should require three main pieces of additional information:
- Where they are located
- How to contact them
- What their issue is

The location information needs to be specific and should include a room or office number, so the technician is easily able to find the end-user. The same thing goes for the contact information. If the ticket can quickly be resolved over the phone or via email, the technician may want a way to reach out to the submitter before visiting. Finally, the problem description field must give the person ample room to explain the issue they are experiencing. When I discuss the work order system with staff members during professional development sessions, I always remind them to be as descriptive as possible. It makes everyone's job much easier when there are plenty of details in the explanation of the issue. Most ticketing systems allow the user to attach a video or a photo as well, but you may need to enable that option. If your system allows it, encourage your users to provide evidence of their problem through images or videos.

With those few data points, your team can take action on a ticket. They now know who is having an issue, what and where that issue is, and how to contact the person with the problem. There is some other information you will want to collect, such as problem category or inventory numbers. I have found it is best not to require these fields. Often the person entering the ticket will select something on the form without thinking too much about it, which can lead to poor data quality and inaccurate analysis.

Accepting Tickets via Email
One feature that is often touted is a system with the ability to receive tickets via email or even social media. When I first heard of systems that could do this, I was excited and intrigued by the idea. After using several that include this functionality, I have lost my enthusiasm for it. Unless the ticketing application is highly advanced, and the email or tweet is formatted in a specific way, the result is a ticket that is missing information. A technician typically has to take the time to adjust the ticket to make it fit correctly into the system. Though this can be considered, it should not be a sticking point when choosing a system.

Notifications

After the user has entered the required information and the ticket has been submitted, they should receive an email from the system acknowledging the work order was received. When one of your technicians updates a ticket to reflect a change, the original submitter should receive an email from the system with the details of the status change. Upon completing a ticket, the end-user should receive an email from the system explaining what actions were taken to resolve their issue.

See a pattern here? After any action is taken related to their ticket, the person who entered the work order should receive an email. The point is to ensure a constant flow of communication advising end-users of the status of their issue. It shows the end-user that you received the ticket and are working on the issue, or that you've solved the problem.

The downside to this design is that the automated emails are often ignored. They are robotic in nature and are usually never read. People may complain that the system sends them too many emails, so they just stopped reading them. There is a solution for this that combines these automated emails with personal ones to create an authentic, customer-friendly experience. See the section on Right Away Reply later in the book.

Don't Delegate

It should be noted that the end user experiencing the issue has to be the one reporting the problem. Self-reporting is highly essential for customer satisfaction and work order completion times. Often times, organizations designate one or two people in each location to enter work orders on behalf of the users. There are a variety of reasons for doing this. Some organizations do not want to burden their end users by asking them to enter tickets. Other times, the IT department does not trust that the end-user can adequately explain the problem.

They appoint tech-savvy people to act as a buffer. This middleman approach creates more problems than it eases in my opinion.

A great example is when the middle man does not create the ticket immediately after the problem is reported to them. Things happen, they get busy, and they do not report the problem for two days. A technician is already forty-eight hours behind in solving an issue that they just heard about. The end-user is frustrated because no one is coming to help them. Another trouble spot that occurs is the middle man's inability to accurately describe the problem because it is not happening to them. Who better to describe the issue they are having than the person having the problem? Finally, when your end users are responsible for reporting their own issues, it creates a sense of ownership on their end. Instead of just telling someone in passing about a concern, they have to take the time to log in and report it.

Let Them See

In addition to submitting tickets, the users should be able to see all the tickets in the system, not just their own. In my opinion, this is a much more important function of the system than most administrators realize. The reason for my belief that everyone should be able to see everything revolves around three things: curiosity, comfort, and transparency. First and foremost, you would be surprised how many people want to see what other users are experiencing. Humans are curious by nature, and it is no different in this situation. Staff members often peruse the ticketing system in a manner similar to how they look at Facebook or Twitter. It is not an in-depth look at every ticket, but they do look to see who is reporting what issues. In my conversations with people about this curiosity, they often mention that they are relieved when they see users who have reported similar problems to their own. It gives them comfort in knowing that they are not the only who is dealing with a particular problem.

Last but not least is the transparency aspect of this design. The information technology industry is complex and mysterious for a significant number of people. When you tell them your department is hectic, they do not have much to go on except your word. They do not understand exactly what it is you do all day. Letting your end-users see one aspect of your workload through the ticketing system is a subtle, but effective, way to handle this issue. Seeing there are fifty, seventy-five, or even a hundred tickets in the queue can be eye opening. They may not understand what needs to be done, but they know whatever it is, there is a lot of it.

Summary
The process to submit tickets must be so easy that anyone in the district can submit one. Barriers to reporting a problem will lead to frustrated users who choose not to report them. If your team does not know about an issue, how can they be expected to resolve it? Along those same lines, you have to create a culture in which submitting a work order is the best way to get a resolution. Empower your users, then reward those users who submit a work order with quick responses to encourage others to do the same.

Technician Side
The technical portion of the ticketing system is equally essential to the end-user aspect. The technicians on your team also need ease of use when working with tickets. It is not that they could not work with a complicated interface, but who wants to? Here are my must-have from the technical side of the ticketing system.

Location Sorting

The system you choose must be able to display open work orders by building. The reasoning is logical enough. Techs typically address work orders based on their location. If you are going to drive out to the Middle School to look at tickets, you will want to know about all the work orders for that building before you ever leave your chair. Additionally, a predefined print out that allows the tech to view information such as name, room number, and ticket details are a bonus.

Reply via Email

We have already discussed that the end-user should be notified via email when a ticket is submitted. All of the technicians should also be notified when a new work order is created. I think you would be hard-pressed to find a system that did not provide notifications by default. The key to those emails is the technician's ability to reply to the notification. A well-designed system is structured in a way that anyone with the initial notification can reply to the email. Additionally, their subsequent response should be automatically recorded as part of the ticket dialogue within the system. The ability to reply via email is an entirely different feature than the accepting a ticket via email one discussed earlier. In my opinion, this is a must-have feature for two main reasons. For starters, it encourages the right away reply method that will be discussed later in this section. The second reason circles back to accountability. I mentioned in an earlier example about the principal who was asking for information about a specific teacher's work order history. Imagine how the principal would react when you presented her with a report of every ticket that was submitted by that teacher along with the associated email correspondence. Many of the available ticketing system options include this as a variation of the feature. I would encourage you to thoroughly test this facet of the application before making a decision.

Categories or Problem Types
The downside to having your end users enter tickets into the system is they do not always know what the real problem is or into which category it should be entered. It's not uncommon for the teacher to make uninformed choices as it relates to the type of problem they have when entering the ticket. This is why categories are important. Categories, or problem types, are a way to classify tickets based on what the root issue is for each ticket.

Part of the process when a tech is closing a ticket should be to verify the correct category has been selected. While your technicians may be eager to close tickets, it is critical that they do so in a thoughtful manner. I will touch on how these categories play an important role in decision making in the administrative section.

Close Your Own
Since we are on the topic of closing tickets, you should ensure that the ticketing system is set up in a way that each technician can close the tickets he/she worked on easily. There are several reasons for having techs close their own tickets. Knocking out work orders is not a glamorous job, but we have all had to do it. Closing tickets is more than just giving credit where credit is due, although that is important. From a technician's point of view, there is a sense of accomplishment when you can log into the system and close out the ten work orders you completed that morning. That feeling only grows stronger when they can look back at how many work orders they have finished in a month or even an entire year. Having access to this summative data can come in very handy on the

administrative side as well. This data can be used as evidence that your department needs an additional technician. On the flip side, it can also stand as factual information when you need to have a tough conversation with a technician about job performance.

One word of caution. Most ticketing systems only allow one person to take credit for the completion of a ticket. Sole ownership can become a problem when multiple team members spend time on a single work order. Who gets the credit for the work? In a highly functional team, your techs will work this out amongst themselves, and you will not need to get involved. Unfortunately, this is not always the case. There may be times when you will need to intervene to ensure tickets are being closed correctly. When there is conflict over who should get credit, here is how I handle it. I listen to both sides of the story to determine who I feel should get credit. On the off chance that I believe they are both correct, I will let technician A close the original ticket. I will then immediately create a second ticket and close it for technician B. It is wise to handle the ticket creation and subsequent closing yourself. You do not want the technicians to begin creating duplicate tickets like this one on their own. The key to success on this particular issue is that you hear both sides of the story and make a fair determination. I do not like this route because it falsely inflates the work order data, but since this is a rare occurrence, I chalk it up to the cost of doing business.

Ticket Status
Quite a few of the technical side suggestions are designed to provide you, as the administrator, with accurate data. This one is no exception. In a black and white point of view, a work order can only be designated as open or closed. A great example of this is a ticket that is waiting for parts to

arrive. A teacher submits a work order for a laptop problem in which it is determined immediately that a new hard drive is needed. A replacement hard drive is ordered, but the part ships from overseas so it is going to take a week to arrive. It does not seem fair that the technical team is going to get saddled with a seven day turnaround time when they have no control over the shipping. The completion statistics will be negatively skewed while waiting for the delivery. The ticket was addressed almost immediately, which should be a win for the department, but the stats will say otherwise. Lucky for us, not everything is black and white.

To help address issues like this, the ticketing system you select should have multiple ticket status options. The options should allow you to configure additional status selection. Almost all of them include options like this already, but you may need to configure them. I only need three status options:

- Open: The ticket stills to be completed. Any time a ticket is set to open, the clock is running, and the time it takes to resolve the issue will be calculated in the administrative reports.
- Closed: The ticket is closed. It is still available in the system for historical purposes.
- On Hold: This is the status I would use for the scenario presented above. The resolution is imminent but is out of your control. It could be due to a back-ordered part or require software that has not yet been purchased. The ticket stays open in the system, however, once its set to On Hold, the clock is stopped and no additional time will be added to the final total.

There are times when a ticket is entered, but it constitutes more than a simple work order. A ticket that is requesting the team re-image an entire lab or something similar would fall into this category. None of the status options above are a fit for such a ticket. In the past, I would create a status called project. In this status, the ticket is closed and no time is calculated through the back end statistics. I would then schedule a time with the end-user for our team to come in and take care of the problem. Nowadays, I delete the ticket and contact the user directly. In my opinion, the project status was flawed because it does not capture all the projects we would do. It only captures those projects that were mistakenly entered into the system.

Resolution Reports
Resolution reports are real-time statistics that show how your team is performing. These reports display data for a predefined period like the current work week or this month. The reported information includes statistics such as average resolution time and the number of tickets completed for the team or individual technicians. The reports can be run on demand and should be customizable to include or exclude various data sets.

The information in these charts are more of an administrative feature, but I feel it is important for the technicians to see the data as well. Most people who take pride in their work like to see how well they are performing over time. Subconsciously, they cannot help comparing their performance to their historical data as well as to that of their peers. It gives them a sense of how they stack up to others. I believe that this encourages people to work a bit harder, knowing that everyone can see how their accomplishments or lack thereof. You have to be careful not to place too much emphasis on these reports. Your staff may begin to take shortcuts or even purposefully dodge phone calls in an effort to preserve high numbers. As the leader, you must set the tone for how this information is perceived. You want your team to know that you do pay attention to the data; however, you also understand that does not provide the whole picture.

In my opinion, a great way to explain it to your staff is that the reports are an excellent form of data to see how the team is operating. Individual team member statistics can be seen as evidence of a potential performance issue, but it will not be the only indicator.

Mobile App

My final" must-have" on the technical side is a mobile app to interface with the system. Technicians need to be able to see up to date information on the tickets that are in the queue. I cannot begin to count the number of times I have gone out to complete tickets in a building based on what was in the system when I walked out the door, only to have additional tickets flow in while I was onsite. Without that immediate, real-time access, I was unaware those tickets had come in, so I left the building without looking at those new issues.

A native app that allows you to interact with the work orders is ideal. I recommend the app route over simple web-based access due to the ease of use on a mobile device. New tickets can be seen as soon as they arrive. Existing tickets can be edited, updated, or closed out in real-time.

Most modern ticketing systems include an app for both iOS and Android, so this should not be an issue. I would be remiss if I did not at least mention this aspect as a criterion based on personal experience.

Administrative Side

From an administrative point of view, all of the data collected by the ticketing system is crucial to measuring the success of the IT department. The most obvious way to measure success is in ticket completion reports. The technology group does much more than just taking care of tickets, right. Why ticket completion is such an important factor in measuring a team's success when tickets are only one aspect of the job. The answer is somewhat apparent if you understand the nature of this industry. Technology is expected to work every single time a user needs to use it. Every time they sit down to send an email, surf the web, or print a report, they expect the devices involved will work flawlessly. Your users do not care about the air-conditioned server rooms, multitudes of universal power supplies, or redundant data centers. When they need something, it better work. When it does not work, the individual gets upset and looks for an immediate resolution. This resolution is where the end-user measures your success. How often do they have problems, and more importantly, how fast does the tech department respond to them? The work order system you choose should be able to track the time it takes your team to complete a ticket down to the second. The importance of accurate information cannot be understated. However, when you are working with the data, there is a saying you need to remember: "Bad data in equals bad data out." Having accurate data is vital in both the short term day to day activities of the department as well as the long-range objectives. Your technicians need to be mindful of that concept as they close tickets. The data collected through your ticketing system will play a significant role in future decisions. Consider the following example:

Kay, in the athletic department, is having trouble trying to get an email to send via webmail. When entering the ticket, she selects email from the dropdown choices because, in her mind, email is the issue. Other options in the dropdown include software install, malware, phone, and hardware which do not appear to categorize her problem accurately. When the technician gets onsite, they discover the issue is related to a malware infection. The infection is quickly cleaned, Kay can send emails again, and the ticket is closed. The problem is that this ticket has an incorrect category associated with it. A miscategorized ticket is often a recurring problem, meaning that closed tickets are not reflective of the actual problem or fix.

Fast forward a few months to a Tuesday afternoon. You are reviewing the data gathered by the work order system to understand better the issues your end users are facing daily. The graphs show that your users struggle most often with your enterprise-level email system. The amount of tickets in the email category outweighs other categories 2-1. Trusting the data you have been presented with, you will likely move in a direction to fix, update, or replace your troublesome email system. You begin prepping organizational stakeholders for a costly upgrade to your messaging platform. However, the actual issue is not email; it is malware. Unfortunately, your data does not back up this fact.

The data categorization can also work against you in another way. The data in the example above incorrectly shows you are having email issues. You know that is not the case, and the problems are related to malware infections. You begin to build a case for purchasing a premium anti-malware software package. When you are asked to justify the cost, the data you have collected does not support your conclusions.
The whole point of gathering all this data is so that you can make an informed decision about the technical issues facing your teachers. I recommend that you review the data with your entire team at the end of every school year. As a group, identify the top three issues that your team spends the most time on or that have affected the highest number of people

(or both). Use category, ticket count, and completion time as your guide. Now that you have pinpointed these problems, determine a course of action to resolve the problems once and for all.

For example, adding printers for staff and students has been identified by the data as one of the top three problems you face. The next step would be to research and discuss potential solutions to minimize the amount of time spent dealing with this issue. Could you modify the login scripts to install printers by location automatically? How about designing a way for users to add their printers? Don't give up on these time-intensive issues that affect a large number of people. Even if you spent several hours or days implementing your solution, it will be well worth it in the long run.

Enter All Tickets
The question of whether or not to have technicians enter every ticket they do into the work order system always comes up when you begin to talk about accurate ticketing data. I have wrestled with the debate for almost twenty years now. The argument surrounds the use of the data once it is entered into the ticketing system vs. the time it takes to enter that data. You should be using that data to analyze your team's effectiveness and to determine which technical issues are monopolizing your technician's time. The only way to be truly accurate is to have all the tickets they have completed, accounted for in the system. This means your techs need to create tickets for every time someone skips the work order process and sends an email asking for help. They will also have to enter a ticket for everyone who stops by the office with a "quick" question.

While your ticket data will be precise, is data entry the best use of their time? You have to account for the time it takes to enter every little password reset or printer jam into the system. Imagine that each technician is spending an hour a week opening tickets and then closing them out right away. Even in a small two-person shop, you are losing upwards of ten hours a week just keeping track of ticket data. How many additional tickets could have been resolved during those ten hours spent entering data?

I do not recommend having your techs enter every single item into the ticketing system. Along those same lines, I also do not recommend letting all of those issues go undocumented either. In every district I have worked in, we have implemented the "five-minute" rule. If it takes a technician less than five minutes to complete the task, it is not worth the time it would take to enter it into the system. Anything more than five minutes of work should be entered, but the goal of the tech should be to get the requester to enter the ticket. For example, a teacher stops by with a laptop loaded with spyware. It takes the technician twenty minutes to clean it up. When the staff member returns to pick up the computer, they will want to login to make sure their equipment is working correctly. Ask them to please place a work order while they are still in the office. This way, you can be sure the ticket is created, but the tech who did the work is not spending the additional time typing it in.

There is one flaw to the five-minute rule. The completion time is not captured correctly. In the example above, the tech spent twenty minutes resolving the issue, but then most likely closed the ticket as soon as it came in. The data captured on that ticket's resolution time will be skewed in your favor. These subtle differences in resolution time do not make a major difference in the overall effectiveness of your department but deserve recognition in this text.

Again, when it comes to the question of whether or not to enter everything into the system, there is not a perfect solution. I have used the five-minute rule for years and found it to be very effective. As with any system, I have challenged my thought process on this particular technique on several occasions to ensure there is not a better way of doing things. The results have always led me back to this method as the most effective way of capturing tickets that were not entered into the system.

Transparency

Transparency works very well for building leaders or department heads as validation of their concerns. I cannot tell you how often I have had the conversation below with another administrator in the district.

- Admin – "Hey, what's the deal with all the issues in my building? I walk down the halls, and all I hear is that we are having major technical issues. What's going on?"
- Me – "Really? I am surprised to hear that. According to the system, there are only a few tickets for your whole building." I'll then open the app, rattle off the issues, and provide an update to each if there is one.
- Admin – "Oh. Ok, let me follow up with my team, and I'll get back to you."

In that conversation, so many positive things have happened for the IT department. For starters, I can confidently dismiss the claim that the building is having major technical issues because I have a system in place to track them. Secondly, by reviewing the tickets and providing a status update, it builds a level of confidence that the technology team is aware of all the reported problems and is working diligently to resolve them. Lastly, it puts the ownership of reporting issues back into the hands of the end-user. If the items are that important, why have the users not taken the time to report them? Remember, the IT department has a user-friendly, easy to use ticketing system in place to ensure staff can easily communicate their technology issues. We cannot solve problems that have not been reported.

Self-Reporting
The final aspect of the ticketing system revolves around creating metrics and the system's reporting engine. We've already discussed the importance of analyzing the data collected by the ticketing system to guide your efforts to alleviate the most common issues within the district. We've also looked at reporting from the technician's side. Now it is time to look at the reporting features from an administrative aspect. From a director's point of view, data is everything.
The system you select needs to have the ability to create and save automated custom reports across a variety of data streams. Use the built-in tools to create reports that measure the team's success. How quickly does your team initially respond to new tickets? How quickly do they close those tickets every month? The measurement increment may be different depending on the system you choose, but I prefer to use minutes for the initial response and hours for the completion metric.   At the end of the month, spend fifteen minutes with your team discussing how the current month compares to the previous month.   If the responsiveness has declined, try to understand what has changed with your team, infrastructure, or organization that has resulted in that decline. Isolate the issue or issues and determine a plan to adjust accordingly for the next month. On the same token, if the responsiveness has improved, define what caused the

increase and celebrate it. For your team to get better, it is crucial to know where they've been. Reporting and discussing the department's progress every month is the best way to accomplish this.

As previously mentioned, I am a huge proponent of transparency, so I provide my administrative team with a copy of the same reports that the technology team sees. We review them and talk about what is going well and what is not. Openly discussing your department's successes and struggles with the superintendent and other district leaders builds trust in your leadership and your team. I strongly suggest you do the same in your district, even if your metrics are not where you want them to be. Often, district leadership only hears about technology when something is going wrong. When things are going well with the department, the leadership team should hear about that too. These reports and your analysis prove that you take your responsibilities seriously. It shows you are striving to develop a robust technology support system for the students and staff.

6
Serving Your Teachers

Let's look at some additional strategies you can use to increase customer service, regardless of the ticketing system you implement.

Right Away Reply
Imagine, for a minute, a system that would immediately and accurately reply to every ticket entered into your work order system with a personalized email directed to the user that addressed their specific issue and provided a timeline for resolution. Your users would be comforted knowing that the IT department received their ticket. The user did not just get the standard automated technical response acknowledging they filled out a form correctly. They would know that a real human being has seen their problem and already has a plan of action to resolve the issue. What a weight off of their shoulders! Someone is going to help them. Think of the confidence that an instant, personal response would build for your department.

I am here to tell you that a system like that exists! You can integrate it with any work order tracking software on the market. It is not software…it is a technician. In fact, it is all of them. Train all of your technicians to treat new ticket notifications with a sense of urgency. You almost want it to be a race to see who is going to call "dibs" on the new ticket first. Even if they are in the field working on other issues, if the distinctive sound of a new ticket breaks in, I argue that they should stop and send a quick response. Think about the time it takes you to read the ticket and craft an immediate response like the one below.

"Hey Jen,

I saw your ticket come through the system about your printer. I'm not in your building today, but I'll stop out tomorrow and take a look.

Thanks
Mike"

It is a simple, two sentence response, but it embodies everything you are trying to accomplish. It starts off addressing the user by their first name. The opening sentence acknowledges that the ticket for her printer was submitted to a real person, not just cyberspace. The second sentence gives a general outlook for when she can expect to see a technician. In less than sixty seconds, the technician has made a positive, personal connection with the end-user and gave her peace of mind that help is on the way.
This system of right away replies can be implemented at any organization regardless of the size. In larger departments, you may want to designate specific individuals to craft and send these replies initially. A traditional help desk with live bodies ready to answer calls can benefit from this as well.

One word of caution: Do not attempt to speed up the process by creating templates that your team can copy and paste into a response. You do not want someone to receive an email that looks identical to one they have gotten from the tech department in the past. You will lose the personal touch that is desired. The email will feel cold and automated, which completely misses the point of these replies.

Email Follow Ups
One fantastic way to change people's perception of your department is to implement a weekly email follow up system. A weekly follow system is a technique that is easy to start, but it is much more challenging to continue. The idea itself is simple. Each week, ask everyone on your team to pick a few work orders that they completed recently. I typically recommend choosing three to five tickets per person to keep it manageable. Now that you have selected some tickets, send an email to the user asking them to confirm everything is still working as intended since you fixed the issue. This should not be a long, drawn-out email. It is a quick, to the point email with one or two sentences verifying the problem is still resolved. See the example below.

> "Good Afternoon Amy,
>
> I wanted to check in to see if you are still able to print from your laptop. I believe I got the problem resolved, but I wanted to be sure it hasn't returned. Please let me know.
>
> Thanks
> Mike"

I cannot begin to tell you what a difference this will make with your users. An email like this shows your end-users that you care about fixing their issues as opposed to just going through the motions. You and your team take pride in your work, and you want confirmation that you have resolved their issue. There are a few more related recommendations to address. First, I recommend that you do not send this for every work order. In my opinion, sending it for every completed ticket can make it feel more automated and less personal. You are trying to build a relationship with your users, so selecting just a few people each week to receive an email delivers a better return. The second recommendation is to remember to choose different people each week. You will want your team to "spread the love" and not just focus these emails on users that they consider friends. In the times I have implemented this, I assigned my staff to the people that I wanted them to touch base with for the first few weeks.

Finally, as I stated above, maintaining this tactic for more than a couple of weeks can be quite tricky. It requires discipline and follow through. As a leader, it will be your job to push your team to keep sending these emails. One way to help is to ask your team to BCC you on each one they send. This provides you a great way to confirm the emails are getting sent. It is also wise to set some time aside each week for your team to compose and send these follow-ups. Setting aside twenty minutes on Friday morning will show your team that this is a priority for you as a manager, so it should be a priority for them as well.

Sorry I Missed You
Often, when a member of the IT staff attempts to resolve an open work order, the end-user is not available. The ticket gets resolved, and the person receives an email letting them know

the problem has been solved. Great, right? Wrong. Many employees frequently ignore work order update emails like they do a SPAM message. Unless the fix is an obvious one (like a new projector bulb), they probably have no idea that their issue has been repaired. They can get frustrated and may accuse you of ignoring them.

A great way to help ensure this does not happen to your team is by using an online service such as Vista Print. Create and print a post-it style note containing the following information.
- Who – A place for your technicians name
- When – Date and time they fixed the issue
- What – A quick note about the problem they corrected
- How – How to contact that tech if the problem is not fixed

Your techs should carry the post-it notes with them as they are doing tickets. If they fix a problem for a user who is not there when they do the work, they legibly fill out the post-it note. Once done, they can post it somewhere that the user is sure to see it. I typically post these in the dead center of their monitor so they cannot use their machine without seeing it. Make sure to purchase something with a sticky back to it.

This technique goes back to the idea that you want to change the perception of your team. People often refer to support technicians as ninjas. One user stated, "They try to slip in and out without you knowing they were ever there." Technicians have the stigma of someone who does not want to interact with people. Tech may be seen as a person who would rather sit behind a desk and work on a computer as opposed to talking to a real live human being. However, in my experience, this is far from reality. These notes are one way to realign those misconceptions.

Raising the White Flag
There are times in this job when you have to give up, plain and simple. It is frustrating and annoying, to say the least. Take an in-depth look at the two most common instances in which you must raise the white flag to signal you have been defeated.

Some problems are just not worth solving. This is more common than many technicians will admit, but it is the truth. For example, a ticket comes in for a machine that is having difficulties staying connected to the wireless network. Several technicians take a crack at it, trying all the standard fixes for such a problem. Updated drivers are loaded, wireless networks are forgotten, and the machine scanned for a variety of malware issues. After several hours, it is finally passed on to the most experienced member of the team. After he/she spends an additional hour wrestling with the problem, there is still no resolution in sight.

In our never-ending quest to fix every single issue that comes across the desk, your gut wants to focus on the question "What the heck is wrong with this machine?" Herein lies the problem, because that is not the issue you should address. The better question is, "Why are we spending so much time on a wireless card?" At this point in the example, at least three people have spent several hours attempting to solve this problem. These types of issues can bog down a department for an entire day or two, preventing technicians from completing other assignments.
Luckily, the cure for this time drain is a very straightforward one. Establish a time limit in your office that dictates how much time a technician should spend on any problem before sending it up the ladder. Additionally, establish a total time

limit on any one issue before you re-image the machine. I recommend you have a thirty-minute limit per technician with a maximum of one hour. Some people would consider this a "cop-out", but that is nonsense. An effective department does not get caught up in problems; it focuses on solutions.

The second common instance is slightly more challenging to navigate. From time to time, a high ranking employee may have the perception that there is something wrong with their computer. Your staff will make multiple visits in an attempt to resolve this phantom issue. These perceived problems are often tough to replicate and highly frustrating. These include system slowness, lock ups, or unplanned reboots. "There's a ghost in this machine I tell ya!" When your team examines the cause, they cannot see anything wrong. The clues tend to gravitate toward something the user is doing, but there is not always a tactful way to say that to someone in a position of power. Honesty will be the key to your success here.

In my experience, the best solution is to give them a new computer. Do you want to? No. Why should you give up a new machine when there is nothing wrong with the current one? In their mind, the present device is tainted, regardless of what you do to it. You could reinstall the operating system from scratch, add additional memory, and spit-shine it to look like it just came out of the box. While it seems new and runs better than before, it is still a lemon to them. This perception can lead to feelings of resentment toward your department or even beliefs of incompetence toward you personally. Swap the computer with a new one or if nothing more, a different one, and save yourself the hassle. When you go this route, make sure, to be honest with the person about your view on the issue.

Example: "While I cannot seem to find anything wrong with this machine, let's go ahead and get you a new computer. Neither of us have time to fight these phantom problems. We'll get one configured immediately for you."

They will feel like you took genuine care of their needs in a special, out of the ordinary way. Your technicians can stop fighting ghostly problems and get back to the real issues that are haunting your machines.

7

ENGAGING YOUR TEACHERS

There is a quote from Winston Churchill that states, "Some people dream of success while others wake up and work at it." It is an inspiring quote meant as a call to action. Do not merely sit back and dream; take control of your destiny. I am sure this quote has been used repeatedly in corporate presentations and motivational speeches worldwide. Over the years, though, the quote has been misstated and misprinted by various individuals and publications. There is a version of it that I prefer to the original text. It reads, "Some people dream of success while others wake up and work."

During my conversations with district IT leaders, engineers, and technicians over the past twenty years, one thing seems to stand out above all else. A vast majority of these individuals do not have a vision. I am not talking about a technical plan for where the district is headed in the next few years. This is not a refresh plan or wireless deployment schedule. I am referring to a goal or a purpose for why they come to work every day; many do not appear to have one. They wake up and go to work. They complete various tasks throughout the day in a futile effort to close every work order and respond to every email. It is considered ineffective because even if they were to close every ticket and reply to every email, new tickets and emails would simply spring up the next day. At the end of the day, they go home, sleep, and start all over with no real goal in mind. How are you supposed to get better at what you do if you do not know what you are working toward?

So what is my goal? Simple: To be a thought leader in educational IT, focusing on customer service and student success. I strive to run the best educational IT department in the nation. I do that by maintaining an open mind, keeping up on educational trends, and listening to what others are doing. That is my personal goal; yours could be very different. That is not the focus of this book; too many other books already cover that specific topic. However, it would be best if you had a professional goal. You cannot expect success just to happen. Set a plan for you and your team, and then develop a strategy to reach that goal. Without one, you are just drifting toward mediocrity.

Be Proactive
In professional sports, the defensive coordinator's job is to read the offense and determine the best scheme to prevent the offense from gaining any ground. This individual must plan a strategy designed to neutralize the offensive threats of the opposing team. They are constantly analyzing data and adjusting their strategy accordingly. As an IT Director, you should employ the same proactive thinking.

I am not just talking about potential threats to the computer or the network. When you think about virus protection, are you thinking about how you will clean up an eventual infection, or are you trying to determine the best way to stop your clients from ever getting infected in the first place? You are obviously going to be proactive and take measures to prevent infections altogether. This visionary thinking extends much farther than just hackers, spammers, viruses, or rootkits. Every aspect of your department should be looked at with a forward-thinking lens.

Consider an example where a lack of forward-thinking could be problematic. The math department has requested a classroom set of iPads for a specialized application designed to help learners struggling with geometry. After speaking with the department head and the building principal, everyone agrees this app and these iPads are the best tools to accomplish the goal. The iPads are purchased using money from your department and the principal's budget as well. Once they arrive, they are deployed. Over the course of the year, the iPads have a positive impact on the students. The kids are learning the material, and you can see proof as test scores begin to rise! Technology is being used to enhance the curriculum. The project is a success.

Now, fast forward five years. The iPads in the math department are in desperate need of being replaced. Out of the original classroom set, only sixteen are still working. Three have cracked screens, and four more will no longer hold a charge. Software updates from Apple have slowed the remaining devices to a crawl, and they cannot even update to the most recent version. The specialized app is still essential to student success, but the most recent release does not run on the outdated hardware. The math department is requesting new iPads. Without proactive thinking, there is no money in your budget to replace them.

Additionally, the high school principal who collaborated on the original purchase is no longer with the district. His predecessor does not know about the initial investment, so there is no money available at the building level either. The result is a frustrated department of teachers and missed opportunities for students. All of this could have easily been avoided with proactive planning when you purchased the devices.

This same proactive thinking mentality applies to more than just purchasing equipment and does not always focus on several years into the future. Consider how your department handles work orders. Are you reactive or proactive? A reactive technology department fixes the issues as they arise, but a proactive department seeks to prevent the problems from ever happening. A real world example of this comes when imaging computers for a large rollout. The reactive approach would be to clone the machines with the department's standard software and administrative settings. The computers are deployed, and any headaches that arise afterward are corrected. This approach can create countless hours of work throughout a single rollout.

A proactive approach attempts to prevent post-deployment headaches by including input from the people who will be using the machines to ensure the most user-friendly image is designed. Let those end users explain the intricacies of what a perfect image would look like for their use. For example, are there settings in Microsoft Word that can be adjusted before creating the image that would make their life easier? Is there a specific application they regularly use that should be included? From there, an image is created with the standard software and administrative settings, along with any additional settings. Then you can clone a few units for testing purposes. Provide these demo units to those same end users to take the newly created image for a test drive. Let them kick the tires for a few days. Technicians should use their feedback to make final adjustments to the master image before cloning all the machines in the rollout. While this may not solve every potential issue that may occur, it goes a long way to preventing additional work once the devices have been imaged. It also shows your teachers that you care about their computing environment. You want to get it right the first time around. Remember, the best offense is a good defense.

Visibility
The department of technology is a mystery to many. They see a world filled with introverted geeks that speak an entirely different language filled with acronyms and inside jokes. It is filled with nerds wearing jeans and comic book T-shirts who spend a large portion of their day sitting behind a computer

screen. For the most part, they know these techs are working on something, but who knows exactly what that might include. When their computer is not working correctly, a tech swoops in, presses a few buttons, and magically the problem (and the tech) disappear.

A successful IT director understands the importance of breaking this stereotype. Here are a few strategies you can use to improve your visibility within the district.

- **Classroom Visits** – A great way to increase your visibility is to spend some time in the classroom, observing how students use technology in your district. This work will change the department's perception; these visits will give you valuable insights into what is working at the point of instruction. You will see firsthand how the teachers are taking advantage of the technology plan you have implemented. I prefer to pop into classrooms without giving the teacher much of a warning if any at all. I believe you will see the most authentic tech interactions with an impromptu visit. Judge the situation, though. If you are a distraction to the learning process, schedule a time with the teacher to come back later.

- **Social Media** – Use social media for more than just school related communication. Connect with your staff via Twitter, Facebook, or Instagram. Let your colleagues see your life outside of the district. Are you taking your kids to the zoo? Post a picture. Just ate at a new restaurant downtown? Tweet about your experience. This is a great way to connect on a personal level. Some people believe you should keep your personal and professional life separate. I think there's a level of private life that can be blended into your professional life without blurring the lines too much. Just like we tell the students, think before you post.

- **Make Yourself Available** – A teacher wanted to teach a lesson using a new web-based application with a classroom full of students. The lesson failed miserably because the site refused to load on a third of the computers. The teacher, obviously frustrated, reaches out to you for advice. Instead of just throwing out some possible resolutions, offer to come out and work one on one with them to fix the problem. You should make time to provide support to those teachers who are willing to make time to try something new.

- **Handle a Ticket or Two** – Similar to making yourself available, do not be too proud to handle a few work orders now and then. I would encourage you to take some time each month to tackle tickets with the rest of the technicians. It helps remind your team you have served your time in a supporting role. You have been in their shoes, and you still know what it is like to work as a technician.

- **Present on Professional Development Days** – Reiterating the point I made earlier, you should be presenting at least one topic, when possible, on your district's professional development days.

Appearance

Appearance goes hand in hand with visibility. A pair of blue jeans with a golf shirt is an acceptable dress code in many professions. In my opinion, Information Technology is not one of those professions. You are a leader. You are directly responsible for leading the Information Technology department. You are charged with making decisions that are research-based, financially sound, and educationally appropriate for your school district. You have a large amount of responsibility on your shoulders. Dress in the attire that says you are the kind of person that can handle that responsibility. The saying goes, "Dress for the job you want, not the one you have." The job you want is a highly respected, intelligent, successful IT director. Does that district administrator I just described sound like he/she wears jeans to work every day? No, I did not think so.

I recommend wearing a suit and tie to your office every day. The suit jacket and tie are a cross-cultural symbol of success. Take a moment to think about how you react when you see someone in a suit. When you walk into a crowded room of people, those wearing a suit typically stand out among the rest of the individuals. The perception is that those wearing a suit are confident, carry a position of importance, and are in control. You want others to know that you are the right person to be leading the district's technology initiatives. Dressing better will go a long way toward that goal.

When you expect to be doing labor intensive work, leave the suit at home for comfortable attire. No one wants to be unboxing computers or climbing in the ceiling tiles looking for a rogue network line in a jacket and tie. Be honest with yourself when making that decision in the morning. On most days, you know what to expect when you walk in the door. Do not use the excuse "Well, I may have to crawl under a desk today" when you know that is highly unlikely.

Approachable
The third key to increasing your visibility in the district is to ensure you are approachable. Approachability is not as easy to achieve as the first two, especially if this is an area that you have struggled with in the past. Once people have the mindset that you are not approachable, it can be tough to change that perception. They may share perceived bad experiences with others, which can strengthen the unapproachable perception.

So what is the best way to increase your approachability? As I mentioned previously, information technology is a customer service industry. To be successful, you need to adopt a customer service mentality to the way you operate your department. It is almost as if you are running your own business and the district staff members are your customers. You are trying to build your department's reputation as a place where people can go to get help.

Many people feel stupid when asking an IT person how to fix a particular issue. They are embarrassed even to ask, especially if they believe the problem is a simple one. Your goal is to make them feel comfortable asking you any technology question, no matter how silly it appears. They need to know that you will respond positively and not ridicule them for their lack of knowledge.

The Open Office model outlined below is a great way to begin establishing that trust with your teachers or build on the reputation you have already created.

Open Office
Set aside an hour every other week for "open office" time. Invite teachers to stop in with any questions they may have so you can work with them individually on their issues. Anything that they want to work on, you are available to help. It goes without saying that when people do stop by, you need to be friendly and willing to assist. If you give the impression that you are being "put out" with their requests, this whole exercise is futile.

Often, the drop in visitors you get will have simple issues that can quickly be resolved. Usually, these issues have been driving them crazy for weeks or even months, and your help will finally resolve them. Once you fix the problem, take a moment to tweet out something positive about what was accomplished.

> "Open office hours have another satisfied customer! @StaffMember can finally get email on her phone. #peskyupdates"

Finally, when you send your reminder to the staff about the open office time, include some of your success stories from the last session. You do not need to be overly detailed. Just mention a few folks who stopped in and how you were able to help them. These emails accomplish three things for you:

- It shows others that the open office hours idea is working. People are coming, and their problems are getting resolved.
- It gives your users the names of people who have already taken advantage of the free time. They can then reach out to those people if they have concerns about how you reacted to their question.
- It helps to show your personal side, similar to what was covered in the visibility section.

Now, rinse and repeat. Offer an open office session, then celebrate its success. As you continue to do this, people will feel more comfortable asking you questions when they see you in the school.

Engage Your Staff

Successful technology directors do more than just research and deploy technology to their staff and students; they encourage its use. You should be empowering teachers to use technology and rewarding the ones who do. If you are not the champion for technology use in your district, then who will be? Creating an environment like this is something that cannot be accomplished overnight. It needs to be fostered and sustained. It needs to be more than just a one-shot installment in a professional development session. I want to discuss an initiative we rolled out this year that succeeded in engaging our staff in the hopes that it better describes what this type of environment looks like.

One of the ways we successfully engaged our teachers was a contest we ran this year dubbed the "21st Century Activities Contest". The contest's goal was to create a fun way to promote new technologies or ideas in the classroom. Simply telling teachers about the tremendous online resources available to them was not enough to spark a change. They needed a legitimate reason to try new technologies to ignite that change. We hoped that a district-wide, yearlong competition might be that reason.

Every couple of weeks or so, we asked teachers to participate in a 21st Century activity with their classes. The dates and activities were posted on a Google calendar so teachers could see what was coming up and have time to prepare if needed. The 21st Century Activities Contest promised a T-Shirt to anyone who completed 80% of the activities. Furthermore, those teachers were entered into a drawing for an additional prize for their classroom, like a new teacher laptop or something similar, of the winner's choosing. Finally, prizes were given out at random times to participants to keep the contest fresh in teachers' minds.

We asked teachers to display their entries on Twitter for two reasons. For starters, entry into the contest required a Twitter account and communication using social media, which we felt was an essential aspect of the 21st-century skill set. Second, we created the custom hashtag #cfevs21 and asked teachers to use it with every post. This allowed us to see everyone who participated in a particular activity, quickly. It also created an easy way to showcase the exciting things that would be happening in the classroom.

The activities below are the first eight we did for the contest. I am not going to dive into why we chose each one, but rest assured, they all had a reason for being selected. I decided to include them in this book using the same or similar phrasing to how I sent them out to the staff if anyone who reads this wanted to re-use them.

- **Activity #1**
  Our first activity is a simple one. Post a question of the week to your Google Classroom website and ask the students to respond. Let us know when you are done by sending out a tweet with the hashtag "#CFEVS21".

- **Activity #2**
  Use a new app or website in your class. This should be something you have not used in the past. It can be a website, iPad app, or Chromebook app. Once you

have tried it out in your classroom, post a short student review of the app or website on Twitter. Don't forget to use the hashtag #CFEVS21.

For Example:
Review: "Soundcloud.com is an awesome app for recording our foreign language assignments."
#CFEVS21

- **Activity #3**
  Our third activity is to "Let the students drive the learning." For this one, the object is simple: Allow the students in your classroom to guide the learning for a subject or class period. As always, take a picture and share it on Twitter with the hashtag #cfevs21.

- **Activity #4**
  The fourth activity for our 21st Century Skills content is to "Integrate Selfies into Your Curriculum." The goal here is to find a creative way to use selfies in one of your lessons. Get creative on this one! Take a few selfies with a curriculum connection and share them on Twitter with the hashtag #cfevs21.

- **Activity #5**
  We'd like you to share those examples on Twitter using a picture collage for the fifth activity. Take some pictures that show how your classroom has changed or how your teaching methods have changed since the Chromebooks were introduced. Once you have the pictures, use an app or website to create a picture collage. Finally, post it to Twitter using the hashtag #cfevs21.

- **Activity #6**
  Our next activity is an excellent way to welcome in the New Year, and it takes only a moment to accomplish. Activity #6 is to tweet out a link to your favorite technology tip on Twitter before next Friday, January

23rd. In your tweet, share a few words on how this tip will help others, and make sure to include the hashtag #CFEVS21.

For example:
"Here's a fantastic way to organize your Google Drive http://mashable.com/2014/11/22/google-drive-organize/

- **Activity #7**
  Activity #7 is to Skype with a class in another district. Setting up a Skype session takes a bit of preparation for both classrooms, so make sure to set a few minutes aside for this. Check out MysterySkype for this. As an added bonus, one person who participates in a Skype session will win a gift for their classroom!

- **Activity #8**
  Browse to the Padlet wall linked below and create a post that showcases something you've done in your classroom that the community should know about. This should be an educational accomplishment, but it does not have to be technology related. Please consider including a picture with your post or a link to a Google Doc that describes the achievement in greater detail. Be sure to include your name on your post as well.

- **Activity #9**
  In her TED talk, veteran teacher Diana Laufenberg discussed the incredible things students had to say once they were given the opportunity. The ninth activity in the 21st Century Activities Contest is to give your students a voice. Create an audio recording on SoundCloud of a student or students sharing what amazed them in class today, what they were most proud of this school year, or what they know now that they didn't know before the year began. Once you've created the SoundCloud, tweet it out for the world to hear. Don't forget to use the hashtag #CFEVS21.

- **Activity #10**
  We are down to the last activity of the 21st Century Activities Contest. Our students have been using their Chromebooks in your classrooms since late August. For the final activity, send a tweet describing how the move to 1:1 computing has changed the way teachers teach, and students learn in our district. There are so many examples I can think of. I am excited to see what you share! Be sure to use the hashtag #CFEVS21 in your tweet.

The contest accomplished what I set out to do at the start of the year. The staff in our district has not been this excited about technology in years. They tried new things and had fun. We had participation in at least one of the activities from close to a third of the teaching staff. In my opinion, the contest was successful because the activities appealed to novice and advanced users alike. They were not overly complicated, and most of them did not require much upfront planning. Best of all, the activities involved the students. It is no surprise that the favorite activity was number four, integrating selfies into your curriculum. Everyone got behind that one. This is just one example of how you can remind your staff that technology does not have to be scary. It would be best to continue to create opportunities to integrate technology, regardless of how you achieve this goal.

This seems to be an area of struggle for technology integration. I get the impression that many directors do not believe this is part of their role in the district. They get too caught up in the job's technical aspects to see the importance of staff engagement. This goes back to my thoughts on using social media, staying visible, and being approachable. You are the champion for technology in your district. What champion does not engage their fans? Get the teaching staff excited to try new gadgets and new ideas! You will be amazed at what teachers will do with a little motivation, especially if they have an integrationist/tech coach to help support when needed and confidence that the technology will work when they go to use it.

8
COMMUNICATION

We live in a world that has become dependent on instant access to information. A world where Twitter provides details on breaking news faster than major news networks. Can you remember a time when you did not check your pocket every time a new email arrived? As a society, we have become accustomed to this constant flow of information. We even get a little uneasy when the flow appears to have stopped. How many times have you looked at your email and thought something might be wrong because you had not received a new message in the past fifteen minutes?

The expectation of rapid communication is increased exponentially for anyone who works in the technology industry. People expect that you have three to five Internet connected devices on you at any given time. Of course, you have seen that email they sent you six minutes ago. Why have you not responded?

Unfortunately, whether you fit that stereotype or not is irrelevant. You are expected to respond to emails, texts, and tweets quickly. I have read many articles and books on personal productivity. Many of them suggest that you only check your email twice a day at predetermined intervals. While I see how that could work well in other professions, I do not recommend it for IT professionals. You do not have the luxury of letting them sit in your inbox for hours or days because folks assume you will get back to them immediately.

Additionally, a certain percentage of your daily emails could be considered tech emergencies to other people. "Help! My projector won't turn on, and I have class next period!". You cannot afford to ignore the constant stream of communication that flows into your office. If you do, the general perception is that you are lazy or you do not care. This is likely a point with which many will disagree. You might think that is not the case at all in your district, that your staff understands how much work is being completed. You are always working, and they have seen your level of productivity. Remember what was discussed in the visibility section a few pages back? The department of technology is a mystery to many people. This fact became very apparent during my time as a consultant.

Often, I sit down with teachers to better understand their view of the technology department. I did this at numerous districts over six years. In the cases where communication was a prominent issue, their perception of busy took on a whole new meaning. The common theme was, "Oh, what? He/She is too busy to respond to a freakin email?!!" Teachers ultimately wrote off the IT director's workload if they could not respond in a timely manner. You have to remember that most people who are not in our profession do not understand what we do all day. What they do understand is that you have not replied yet, and that is creating an issue for them.

My suggestion is to develop a system for reading and responding to emails. You want a system that satisfies the immediate response requirement but does not lead to your inbox controlling your day. The way I handle this is through a series of simple rules for email.

1. When a new email arrives, if you can respond to it quickly, with a few words or a sentence, do that right away. If not, the email probably requires you to do something other than just reply. Flag or star that email to be answered later.

2. Make time in your day for email. During those times, sort your email by putting the flagged ones at the top. You can then begin replying to only those emails you determined require action on your part. It creates a mini To-Do list in your inbox, which I find to be very helpful.

3. Do your best to reply to every email the same day it arrives. Even if the reply is something like, "I wanted you to know that I saw this email but haven't had a chance to get it yet." This way, you acknowledge you have seen their email and will get back to them. It helps to ease any concerns over a lack of response.

When it comes to responding to emails, try to provide relevant information without being long-winded. In my opinion, the longer the email, the less likely people are to read it all the way through. Staff members may begin to think you have too much time on your hands if you continually send out multi-paragraph emails packed full of information that most do not care about.

For example, if the network goes down in the district, most people do not care if your DHCP server malfunctioned and started passing out duplicate addresses. They do not need a lesson on IP addresses, subnet masks, and network protocols. All they want to know is there was a problem, it has been taken care of, and it should not happen again. Your email to the staff should read:

> "The network was down today for approximately 30 minutes starting at 1:00 pm. The issue has been corrected and should not be problematic going

forward. We apologize for any inconvenience this may have caused."

Lastly, be thoughtful about your replies. When you respond to an email, your goal should be to get everything you may need with that person's response. Everyone already gets too many emails, so you want to avoid creating the need for multiple emails to be exchanged. Additionally, it can slow the process down significantly if you are continually waiting for replies. Here is an example of what I mean:

A user sends you the following email:
> "I came in this morning and seemed to have crazy pop-ups no matter what I open. I will not need it most of this morning. I'll have one of my students drop it off in your office. Can you check my computer, please?"

A typical response might look like this:
> " Sure. I'll take a look and let you know what I find."

You agree to look at it, and then you will let the person know what you can do to correct the problem. The problem with that response is that it already suggests the need for additional emails to be exchanged. How are you going to let them know? Most likely via email. Once they read your diagnosis, they will either reply with a thank you or have to answer additional questions you have to ask them based on what you find. Depending on the severity of the issue, you may need to wipe the machine, so you will have to ask if they have backed up their stuff, if you can keep it longer than the morning, and if they need anything special installed after you are finished.

You may want to login as the user and do not know their password in some cases. This is yet another email or phone call. All of the back and forth will drag the process out more than necessary.

My suggestion is to have a few canned responses that you use in these situations. Here is an example of a reply designed to save time and gather all the information you may need upfront.

> For example:
> "I'd be happy to take a look at your laptop. Every malware or virus infection is unique. They all cause different issues depending on what they have managed to infect. This could be a quick fix, or it could be much more severe, but I won't know anything until I can look at it. To ensure I can get your computer fixed as quickly as possible, please answer a couple of questions first.

> 1. Are the documents, spreadsheets, pictures, videos, and other important files on this computer backed up somewhere safe?

> 2. Do you have any special software loaded on the computer? i.e., Photoshop, Smart Notebook, etc.?

> 3. If the problem is severe, the computer may need to be wiped clean, and everything reinstalled. The process can take several hours or longer. If that is the case, will you need a loaner computer?

> 4. Lastly, a technician may need to log in to the computer as you to verify the problem has been resolved. Can you please provide your network password? If you are not comfortable giving this out over email, please call us at ext xxxxx."

To recap the last few pages, communication from the IT department should be quick and ongoing. Every team member should strive to answer emails in a timely fashion, never letting them go more than a day without a reply. They should be efficient but not long-winded. Do your best to avoid generating multiple back and forth messages without sounding robotic in your interactions. Your emails should still have a personal side to them. Lastly, know your audience. You are communicating with a large group of educators, not a technical support team. They do not care much about the technical details. They want to know you have things under control. Creating a well written, efficient email is a true art form. While I have composed hundreds of thousands of them over the years, I am continually looking to refine my craft.

Digital Police
At a recent edtech conference, I was having a debate with a colleague from another school district. To provide a bit of a back story, I have known him for many years. I respect the work he has done over that time to move his district forward. On many issues, we share the same viewpoint. This one, though, was a different story. We fundamentally disagreed on what most would consider a minor issue. So why write about it? Since I have had this "battle" far too many times with far too many different people.

The topic was whether teachers and students should know the password to the school's wireless network. The argument at its core boils down to a control issue. As an IT leader, you want to control every device that attaches to your network. By keeping that password under lock and key, you prevent any external devices (or devices unknown to you) from connecting. This, in turn, helps guard against virus attacks, hacking attempts, and general wireless misuse.

While this idea of total control does hold some weight, in my opinion, it is an outdated way of thinking. Keeping the password a secret leads to LESS control in the end. The increased access to the Internet via smartphones has made access to your local district provided Internet less important. Why use the school's access when I can use my data plan? The result is many students and teachers surfing the web on personal devices, unbeknownst to you. Where is the control in that? Taking the control aspect off the table for a minute, think about the additional challenges you face when you keep the password a secret:

- Changing the password if it does leak and discovering who leaked it.
- Additional work orders to enter the password for people who do need it.
- Dropping everything to handle guest presenters who require network access that you didn't even know were coming to your district.

As a technology director, your role in today's educational system is to provide access to the vast resources available on the Internet, not prevent it. The wireless password should be posted on signs throughout your buildings, encouraging people to join your network. You have built this fantastic wireless network to handle all the increased access required for things like BYOD, 1:1, and state assessments. Your wireless access is far superior in both speed and reliability to what those folks have on their LTE data plans. It would help if you used this as a way to entice them back onto your network; your filtered, monitored, controlled network. When the vast majority of your users connect through your network, you will have an excellent idea of what device is going where and what it is being used.

Furthermore, your department will spend less time dealing with the access related issues outlined above. Staff and students will be grateful to you for the speedy access and for saving their personal data. In summary, by promoting access to your district's wireless network, you will gain the control you desire by openly displaying the password while decreasing your workload.

Content Filtering
The same openness applies to how you approach Internet content filtering. In most districts, this is the control over whether a site is accessible within the school buildings. There are quite a few factors that must be considered when

determining the policy on sites like YouTube: School and community culture, students' awareness of digital citizenship, and technology access, to name a few. With all of that being said, my personal opinion is that it comes down to how your district administration views technology's role in education. Do they understand that students of today learn differently than we did when we were growing up? Kids look to sites like YouTube for more than just entertainment. They learn from these sites by listening to their peers describe the problem at hand and then watching them solve that problem in their own unique way.

Remember this same issue from when we were growing up. I think back to a staple of 80's pop culture: The Karate Kid. Two-thirds of the way through, the Karate master and teacher, Mr. Miyagi, can be seen practicing a special "crane" kick on the beach. Daniel, the student, watches on from a distance. He later uses that same kick to defeat the bad guy in the Karate tournament championship match, earning a first-place trophy, respect from the bullies, and the girl. What a classic movie! Here is the lesson, I remember how many times I went out in the back yard and secretly practiced that crane kick. You know you did too! Standing on one leg with your arms out at your sides (trying to look cool) was already hard. When you add that there were no instructions in the movie on performing the legendary move, it became almost impossible to truly get it right. I do not know about you, but I tried often, failed just as often, and eventually moved on to more incredible things, like creating a time-traveling Delorian using the family Toyota. Now imagine that YouTube had existed in 1984. I would have watched every video I could find detailing how to pull off a perfect crane kick. Wouldn't you? That is the difference between kids now and when we were in school. Students have access to an ever-expanding world of information. Why would you ever want to limit their access to that, especially at the institution where they go to learn?!

I am not suggesting that you remove the content filter entirely, but the days of blocking sites like YouTube and Twitter are gone. Sure, like many social media sites, there is some inappropriate material at times. Still, both services offer such an incredible amount of high-quality content that blocking them seems ridiculous. Besides, even if you choose to block sites like that, your student population will simply use their smartphones to access it anyway. When I look at unblocking a site, I ask myself, "What's the potential for educational value in this site?" Assuming the site can provide that educational value and it is not related to pornography, gambling, illegal activities, or hate speech, I will typically unblock it. In the past five years, I can only recall one instance where I did not open a site. It was nothing more than a torrent site disguised as a legitimate resource.

Remember, your goal is to build bridges, not barriers.
- Open up your wireless to district stakeholders.
- Relax your content filtering policy.
- Encourage students and staff members to use social media appropriately .

9
Budgeting

Technology Planning Sessions

Creating a purchasing plan, implementing that plan, and maintaining the technology for your district is a significant aspect of your role as Director of Technology. It can be one of, if not the most, challenging parts of your position. I used to think that since I know technology better than anyone else in the room, I know what is best for them. Over the years, I have come to respect the process of making these decisions much more than I did early on in my career. You are making decisions that will affect how students learn.

Planning session conversations should focus on the expected outcomes, not on vendor specific devices. All too often, teams get wrapped up in what a particular device can or cannot do. Someone wants to buy iPads because of an app they saw at an edtech conference. Others do not want to consider Chromebooks because they do not run Microsoft Office. It can be challenging to keep the device out of those talks, but you have to let the outcomes drive the selection process. This can be hard for members of the selection team who really like one specific device, but in the end, this process should show you the device that will accomplish the majority of your desired outcomes.

The budget should also mostly be kept out of these initial planning conversations. Yes, at some point, the amount of money you have available will determine how much of the plan can be implemented and in what year. Cost is a constraint, but don't let the dollars drive the decision. Again, focus your efforts on student outcomes. You can even ask the planning team members to dream a little bit. Spark the conversation by asking them to design the perfect classroom if money wasn't a factor.

The perspective outcomes you design should have an emphasis on skills, not on particular software or applications. For example, an outcome such as "Must run Raz-Kids software" should not make the list. You should not make a large purchase based on a particular application unless that application is the whole reason for the purchase. Some examples of more desirable outcomes include "Increase student collaboration," "Multimedia content creation," and "Increase typing proficiency."

One suggestion would be to write out all of the desired outcomes on a whiteboard or spreadsheet. Once you have completed that, create a column for each device to the right. Now go through each outcome and determine whether the device will support that specific outcome.

Outcome	iPad	Chromebook	Surface	Laptop
Increase student collaboration	Yes	Yes	Yes	Yes
Multimedia content creation	Yes	Yes	Yes	Yes
Increase typing	Yes	Yes	Yes	Yes

proficiency					

The end result should show you the device that will accomplish the majority of your outcomes. However, depending on the project's scope and the size of the team creating the outcomes, choosing a winner based on the majority may not be the most effective method. It is the classic battle of quantity vs. quality.

Outcome	Weight	iPad	Chrome	Surface	Laptop
Increase student collaboration	5	No	Yes	No	Yes
Multimedia content creation	3	Yes	Yes	Yes	Yes
Increase typing proficiency	2	No	Yes	No	Yes

For larger projects, consider weighting the desired outcomes. Ask each team member to select a numerical value between 1 and 10 for every goal listed. Gather their responses, add up the collective weight for each outcome, and then get the average by dividing the score by the number of team members who participated. Next, place the average in an additional column in the spreadsheet. Finally, calculate each overall score by adding the rows where the device received a "Yes" vote. When all is said, and the scores are tallied, the selected device is the one that is going to accomplish the most highly rated outcomes.

This framework is suitable for more than just selecting a device for student use. You can apply this same methodology when choosing classroom technology (Smartboards, document cameras), software packages, and even copiers.

One thing this framework does not take into account is consistency at the building level. Using this framework might lead to different results at different grade levels. An outcome weighted heavily for high school students may not even play a factor for elementary students. This becomes difficult because from the technical side of the house, supporting different devices for each building or grade level can be overwhelming, if not impossible, depending on the district's size. From the academic viewpoint, though, you just completed an exercise that resulted in different devices based on the desired outcomes.

Device selection can be a difficult sticking point for the group to maneuver. A perfect example is the debate over 1:1 computing that is currently occurring. As previously mentioned, most districts are not engaging in conversation over whether or not to go with a 1:1 model. They have already determined that is the route they will take within the district. The question revolves around what device will take the district in the desired direction. There are many highly successful initiatives using Chromebooks, but districts have accomplished their goals using iPads or Surface tablets. The truth of the matter is that regardless of what device you select, the success comes from implementing it with the students, communicating it to the parents, and supporting it with the staff. Do not let the device drive the conversation. Determine your outcomes first; everything else comes afterward.

Budget Creation

Creating a budget to guide and track the department's spending is a massive part of the planning process. During my years as a consultant, I was amazed at how many directors I spoke to that did not handle this aspect of the job. These directors found themselves in a never-ending loop of financial problems. In most of those situations, the inability to create a budget led to an underfunded technology department with little to no control over their finances. The district was hesitant to fund an account or plan that was not sustainable or did not include a forecast. The lack of financial control, in turn, contributed to the future creation of inadequate technology plans. When the yearly budget cycle came around, the poorly designed technology plans reaffirmed the department's lack of trust, ensuring another year of insufficient funding. As the years went on, the CTO did not replace the district infrastructure in a timely manner. Eventually, a sizable, one-time injection of money was required to upgrade the infrastructure to an acceptable manner but failed to address sustainability issues. Subsequent funding would return to inadequate levels because "we just gave you all that money a year ago," and the cycle would start all over again.

Budget creation should be done using a systematic approach, in a manner that allows you to forecast future years with ease. When creating the budget for the upcoming school year, costs should be divided into two main sections:

- **Recurring Costs** – costs that the district will incur year after year, much like the electric bill. Typically this would include things like software licensing, maintenance agreements, and ITC costs.

  To develop this portion, the IT department should create a list of all the recurring costs that the department pays. Once that list is generated, the CTO should contact the vendor for each line item to verify that the price has not changed. This process is also an excellent time to record when each software package is due to be renewed. Recording those dates can help prevent accidental license expirations or unintended renewals.

- **Project Costs** – costs associated with that year's projects which came from the district technology plan. While evaluating project costs, it is also essential to identify which project costs will become recurring costs in future years and which costs are one-time costs.

  As stated above, start this section by reviewing the technology plan to see what is slated for the upcoming school year. Now, check those projects to ensure they still fit with where the district is headed. Remember, the technology department's plan must be in alignment with the district's strategic plan. The IT staff should discuss any unplanned projects as well. Lastly, are there any programs from the state that require technology? (All day kindergarten or online testing, for example).

The educational technology leader should set a small amount of the budget aside for unexpected issues. Some examples include a failed network switch, a batch of lousy projector bulbs, or an unanticipated software application.

Finally, some money should be made available for R&D. The IT department is supposed to be the district leader for all things technological. When a device or application is released, they should have some freedom to purchase it. There is no question that they will be asked about the cool new toy on the block, so in fairness to them, they should have a chance to take one or two for a spin.

Sample Budget

Recurring Costs	Cost Estimate
All Call System	$4,500.00
Web Site	$5,100.00
Onboarding Application	$1,500.00
Substitute Management System	$1,330.00
DataWarehouse	$4,290.00
Credit Recovery System	$12,700.00
Microsoft Office	$7,875.00
Gradebook	$20,000.00
Student Information System	$15,000.00
Internet Connectivity	$12,348.00
Peripheral Devices (Printers, Digital Cameras, Projector Bulbs)	$10,000.00
Printer Supplies, Parts and Toner	$20,000.00

Staff Development	**$5,000.00**
Computer Components	**$20,000.00**
Outside Consultants	**$1,200.00**
TOTAL	**$140,843.00**

Project Costs	Cost Estimate
Teacher Laptop Refresh	**$97,000.00**
Security Server SAN	**$15,000.00**
Stadium Internet Access	**$6,000.00**
New Document Cameras	**$1,500.00**
Counselor Tablets	**$900.00**
Unexpected Repairs	**$10,000.00**
R&D	**$3,000.00**

	TOTAL	$133,400.00
	TOTAL	$274,243.00

Budget Categories

One helpful exercise when creating the budget is to divide your spending into categories. I do this on almost every budget I create, regardless of whether it is for the upcoming school year or a multi-year plan. This exercise aims to ensure that every aspect of the network is being considered during the financial planning phase. It should help a district avoid a situation where one or more parts of the system become detrimentally outdated, while others get too much attention. In my opinion, there are seven categories in which IT purchases can fall. To complete this project, you simply assign each of your budgeted purchases to one of these seven groups. When that is complete, use a pie chart to illustrate what you plan to spend on each category.

Infrastructure - This includes anything related to the data or voice infrastructure. (Switches, routers, access points, UPS devices, VOIP phones, etc.)

Access - Laptops, tablets, desktop PCs, and other devices purchased for staff or student access to information.

Classroom -This category is designated for equipment used for classroom instruction such as projectors, smartboards, document cameras, etc.

Software - Use this group for all software purchases, including academic applications, operation applications, and technical software purchases.

Security - Physical (cameras and equipment that relate to security across the district) and virtual (cybersecurity applications and appliances for keeping the district safe).

Printing - This group is for printers and all associated costs such as toner or spare parts.

Development - This category is labeled for funds set aside for professional development opportunities, as well as any equipment purchased for research or trials.

There are a few things to note about this activity. For starters, some purchases could be assigned to multiple categories. In those cases, use your own judgment on the best group in which to allocate the cost. Just remember to follow the same logic for other purchases as well in additional years. You do not want to assign a price to access one year and then software the next, or it will skew the results. There may be a few items that do not appear to fit into any category along those same lines.

A perfect example is the money set aside for parts and repairs of various district systems. It does not fit well into those categories, but it does not deserve a group of its own. You can similarly treat these as you did the things that could fit into multiple categories. Either assign the item to the group that works best or leave it out of the graph altogether. Whatever you do, continue to do the same with that purchase in future years.

Using the example budget above, I categorized each item using the seven groups and a few exclusions.

Recurring Costs	Category	Cost Estimate
All Call System	Software	$4,500.00
Web Site	Software	$5,100.00
Onboarding Application	Software	$1,500.00
Substitute Management System	Software	$1,330.00
Data Warehouse	Software	$4,290.00
Credit Recovery System	Software	$12,700.00
Microsoft Office	Software	$7,875.00
Gradebook	Software	$20,000.00
Student Information System	Software	$15,000.00
Internet Connectivity	Infrastructure	$12,348.00

Peripheral Devices (Printers, Digital Cameras, Projector Bulbs)	**Classroom**	**$10,000.00**
Printer Supplies, Parts and Toner	**Printing**	**$20,000.00**
Staff Development	**Development**	**$5,000.00**
Computer Components	**Excluded**	**$20,000.00**
Outside Consultants	**Infrastructure**	**$1,200.00**
TOTAL		**$140,843.00**

Project Costs	Category	Cost Estimate
Teacher Laptop Refresh	**Access**	**$47,000.00**
Photography Lab Refresh	**Access**	**$30,000.00**
Programming Lab Refresh	**Access**	**$20,000.00**
Security Server SAN	**Infrastructure**	**$15,000.00**

Stadium Internet Access	**Infrastructure**	**$6,000.00**
New Document Cameras	**Classroom**	**$1,500.00**
Counselor Tablets	**Access**	**$900.00**
Unexpected Repairs	**Excluded**	**$10,000.00**
R&D	**Development**	**$3,000.00**
TOTAL		**$133,400.00**
TOTAL		**$274,243.00**

At this point, you have categorized the majority of your spending. Now take the data and graph it into a pie chart, as I have done below. This chart shows that a vast majority of the money allocated to this year's budget will be spent on student and staff devices for access to information, while no money is being used for security. In the short term, there is nothing wrong with one or two categories monopolizing the funds. The intended use of this exercise is not to have a perfectly proportioned pie chart. It is designed for you to take a look at a graphical representation of your proposed spending. As I stated previously, this activity's goal is to ensure that every aspect of the network is being considered during the financial planning phase. This view can be constructive when you graph several years of spending side by side. Those pictures will paint a picture of the pattern of spending habits and show aspects of your network that need attention.

Refresh Planning

A refresh plan is a replacement schedule used to forecast when equipment will need to be replaced to ensure the end-user can continue to perform their job duties at a high level. In layman's terms, it is a plan for replacing technology before it becomes too old. Designing the initial refresh plan for a district can be challenging, but once you have completed a full cycle, creating a new plan is more straightforward. The challenge for the initial plan is both financial and technical. From the technical side of things, you first need to determine what devices you will put on a refresh plan. When I am working to figure this out, I create categories of equipment that I believe need to be replaced regularly. Typically, this includes four major groups: Teachers' computers, Administrative computers, Support staff computers, and Lab machines. You may have some other groups to think about, depending upon your district's makeup. Once you have decided what to replace, you need an accurate inventory of those devices being used, including the age of each machine. You will use this data to determine what machines to replace and what machines to shuffle around to new spaces throughout the district.

During this initial refresh cycle, the trickle-down will become your best friend. Trickle-down is the process of using newer machines from one location to replace aging machines in another site. This is not a substitute for purchasing new machines for those aging devices. It is merely a way to make computing a little better for those areas that may not see new machines until the end of the refresh cycle. We will look at this more in the real world example below.

The other challenge I mentioned is related to school funding. For a refresh plan to work correctly, the district must commit the necessary monies to complete the cycle over a predetermined number of years. During the initial rollout, the technology budget may need to see some additional funding to implement the plan correctly. You will need to work closely with your superintendent and treasurer to secure the funding for the plan's length, not just the first year or two.
Over the past two decades, I have been responsible for creating successful equipment refresh plans for numerous school districts, ranging in size and all with different financial variables. It is through those years of experience that I designed the Golden Year Model.

Golden Year Model

The purpose of the golden year model is to systematically replace the selected devices within your budget's confines while leaving room for the unexpected. We will use a four-year refresh cycle for this book's purpose, but this model does work in a five-year process. The four-year model is based on the assumption that the district can expect four years of useful life from the device in the role for which it was purchased. This doesn't mean the device needs to be thrown away when that period is up. It merely means that it will be replaced with a new model while serving the district in a secondary role. To accomplish this, we will spread the cost of the devices over three years, not four. The fourth-year is what I call the golden year, but we will get to that later.

The key to a well-designed refresh plan includes more than just a fiscally responsible methodology. You need to be sure to distribute the wealth among as many buildings or grade levels as possible. Pouring all your money into a few buildings each year can quickly lead to frustration. No one wants to support a plan that does not do anything for their building until the very end, regardless of its fiscally sound.

Review this realistic example of the golden year model in action. The district in question had three main goals with a four-year timeline:

- Provide every staff member with a new laptop within three years.
- Increase wireless access across the district.
- Replace every lab across the district with new equipment at the same time.

Before getting started, you will need to identify the location and approximate age of the equipment that will be replaced. This is a vital aspect of any refresh project. You may not always replace the oldest technology first, though, as you will see in this example. The existing layout for our functional district is as follows:

Description	Count	Age (in Years)
Teacher computers	200	Varies
Additional Computers	20	Varies

GTT Lab at the Middle School	25	6
PLTW Lab at the High School	25	5
Library Lab at the High School	30	5
Library Lab at the Middle School	30	5
Lab at Garfield	27	3
Lab at Lincoln	27	3
Lab at Hayes	27	3
Lab at Washington	27	3
Science Dept Lab at the High School	32	3
Technology Academy Lab at the High School	30	3
Science Dept Lab at the Middle School	32	3
Language Arts at the Middle School	30	2

Year One

The first year of the refresh plan should directly affect the most number of users, especially if there has never been a formal plan in place. For this district, providing new laptops to the High School and Middle School and increasing wireless access at those buildings was the most effective approach. Also, I recommend replacing the labs in the four elementary buildings. This will guarantee that those teachers have access to a lab with reliable technology for their students. This purchase should build some goodwill with those teachers since they will not be receiving new laptops in the first year.

The CTO should use the existing computers at the four elementary buildings to replace the following five and six year old labs:

- GTT Lab at the Middle School
- PLTW Lab at the High School
- Library Lab at the High School
- Library Lab at the Middle School

While these are not new machines, they are more recent than what is currently being used. Using this trickle-down model, coupled with a software package like Deep Freeze, should create a dependable computing environment for those labs.

	Count	Cost	Total
Teacher Laptops at the HS	50	$799	$39,950
Teacher Laptops at the MS	50	$799	$39,950
Increase Wireless Access (w/o installation)	75	$500	$37,500

New Labs at Four Elementary Schools	120	$650	$78,000
Total Cost			$1 95,400

Year Two

Year two of the refresh plan continues with the increase in wireless access across the district. The district should look at a more robust wireless implementation at the four elementary locations. It may not be a full wireless deployment, but it will give wireless access to most classroom teachers. Along with the wireless, the district should purchase laptops for the teachers at those buildings. The focus should be to replace the Science Department labs at both the Middle School and the High School for the labs.

	Count	Cost	Total
Teacher laptops at Garfield	24	$799	$19,176
Teacher laptops at Lincoln	22	$799	$17,578
Teacher laptops at Hayes	28	$799	$22,373
Teacher laptops at Washington	26	$799	$20,774

Increased wireless at those 4 buildings (25 per)	100	$500	$50,000
Lab replacements	64	$650	$41,600
Total Cost			$17 1,501

Year Three

The refresh plan's final phase wraps up the replacement of labs, staff computers, and any additional wireless expansion that was not affordable in the previous years. The third-year also takes into account the uncertainty of IT and school funding. Any projects that were not completed in the first two years can be addressed.

	Count	Cost	Total
Additional Computers	20	$799	$15,980
High School Library	36	$650	$23,400
Middle School Library	33	$650	$2 1,450
GTT Lab at the Middle School	32	$650	$20,800

PLTW Lab at the High School	24	$650	$15,600
Technology Academy Lab at the High School	30	$650	$19,500
Language Arts Lab at the Middle School	30	$650	$19,500
Additional Wireless Access	30	$500	$15,000
Total Cost			$1 51,230

Year Four (The Golden Year)

At the end of three years, the district had installed a wireless network in every building, provided every staff member with a new laptop, and replaced all of the labs with new computers. This design's beauty is that it is a four-year refresh cycle, but the CTO accomplished everything in three years. That is the ultimate goal. Design the refresh for four years, and then complete it in three. This does not mean you are only expecting three years of useful life out of the equipment. You should still expect four full years of good use, if not more. What makes this so special is that nothing needs to be refreshed in the fourth year. Nothing! The CTO can use the fourth year's budget to complete significant projects such as creating a fabrication lab or upgrading the network infrastructure. You could also consider using the fourth year to tackle those behind the scenes issues, those things that get cut from the budget on an annual basis because there is always something more important to address. Whatever you chose to do with the money, the point is that it is available.

When this model was initially designed, the intent was never to have an extra year of open spending. It was a four-year refresh plan that was to be completed in four years. Other districts were implementing similar models using either a four or five-year life cycle. The problem in my eyes was that you were always replacing equipment. When it came time for a system-wide project like upgrading the infrastructure, you had to ask for additional funding. Completing the refresh in a shorter time frame allowed some financial breathing room for the unexpected. I do not believe this refresh model to be innovative. However, it is a better method than what the other districts were using.

Methodology
In this example, the question I hear most often is what about consistency. Looking at my design, you will more than likely be ordering different model laptops each year. You could potentially be ordering different access points as well. Why not just order all the laptops in the first year? Then the access points in the second? Everything would be consistent. Consistency can be both a blessing and a curse, specifically when it comes to staff devices. My argument against doing a refresh that way is twofold. First of all, you are setting yourself up to replace every single laptop four or five years after your initial order. Right off the bat, that is a substantial financial commitment in the school funding cycle that always seems to be in flux.

Additionally, you can expect some very unhappy teachers during that last year or two when they are working on five year old laptop. Some applications will not work due to age, while other machines will simply not make it all five years. You will have to determine a way to replace them, most likely with new computers. You will be shocked at how many "dead" laptops you will have at your door when the staff sees someone with a new computer because theirs stop working. The final design of the refresh project is up to the architect of the plan. The example above shows one method that has worked very well for me in the past. However, there always seems to be more than one way to get the desired results when it comes to technology.

10
Failing Forward

The vice president of the consulting firm I worked for once asked me about failure. I promptly replied, "I never fail." What an overconfident, ignorant thing to say, right? He looked at me with a very puzzled look and politely replied, "Really? I fail all the time." before walking away. That small interaction stuck with me over the next few days. The individual leading my division and making significant strategic decisions for a multimillion-dollar organization openly admitted that he routinely failed. Aren't leaders supposed to be highly educated individuals paid not to make mistakes? After quite a bit of research, reading, and contemplation, I came to discover that we viewed failure differently. I viewed failure as the opposite of success. He viewed failure as a growth opportunity. The difference is that he studied every failure and adjusted his efforts based on what he had learned. On the other hand, I rarely examined the root issue of why I had not succeeded outside of the technical aspects. Do not get me wrong; I did learn from my mistakes, but not in a thoughtful manner.

Technology professionals can be stubborn people. We find something that works well, and we stick to it. The ironic thing about this group of tech enthusiasts is that even with the constant stream of innovations that occur, we still do things a particular way because that is how we have always done them. I would bet there are things you do in your daily routine only because it is the way you first learned how to do it. You never consider changing your methods because "if it ain't broke, don't fix it."

Now that I understand failure, my philosophy is more like, "If it ain't broke, is it the best?" By that, I mean even though something is working well, could there be a better way to complete the process? I am always looking for new ways to perform routine tasks to be more efficient. In some cases, I stumble upon a unique solution that never crossed my mind or an application that can help accomplish my goal. I then implement the idea and find that it cuts minutes or hours out of a process. Other times though, I move forward with a new concept that backfires altogether.

For example, I was looking for a solution to prevent staff members from getting malware before a recent laptop deployment. Looking at the work order data, it was clear that we were spending too much time cleaning up or imaging infected laptops. I needed to find a way to reduce the amount of time we spent on those devices. Logically, I wanted to develop a plan to prevent unwanted applications from being loaded on the laptop. At the same time, I tried to maintain their administrative level access to the machine so they could install applications without asking our department to do it for them. I explored several antivirus/antimalware solutions without finding one that blocked the unwanted programs to the extent needed. I decided to take a different route altogether. We used a package on our lab machines that reset the system back to the frozen state upon every restart. I modified the package for the staff laptops to freeze the system drive while leaving their user profile untouched. We deployed on the package about sixty brand new laptops. It worked well for the first few days, but then problems began to arise, lots of them. The idea was a complete disaster and created quite a bit of work to clean up.

To quote Thomas Edison, "I have not failed. I've just found 10,000 ways that won't work". I do not look at the freezing idea as a failure. It is just an idea that did not work. I learned more from that mistake than just the obvious. I realized that I could not have the best of both worlds. If I want to allow our teachers to use their devices with few restrictions, some are bound to get infected with unwanted malware. I needed to adjust my strategy to account for this unfortunate fact. Since I would not be able to completely stop the potential infections using this software, I needed to do a better job educating everyone on how to avoid possible malware infections. For those machines that still managed to get infected, I needed to figure out a faster way to remove the infection or wipe the machine. While I am still working on refining the process, the amount of time spent on those devices has dropped dramatically this school year.

If you do not take the time to understand what specifically caused you to fail, how can you expect to learn from it? In the example above about the laptops, understanding why the plan did not work was more about the underlying issue of end-user development and my beliefs about laptop privileges than it was about any technical malfunction that occurred. By taking the time to isolate the real cause, I could get a better handle on the next steps. Instead of attacking the problem with another malware scanner or application, I am approaching it from an entirely different angle.

Like most people, I do not set out to fail. However, when failure occurs, I will openly admit the mistake. I will also spend the necessary time identifying what did not go well and how I can move forward.

Summary

This book focused on the areas that I believe are the keys to a high performing IT department in public education. The first is a technical team focused on customer service—one made of extroverts who understand the value of relationships with colleagues and staff members from other departments. The second key to success is a well-designed ticketing system collecting data behind the scenes. Teachers know to use the system to receive quick, reliable support. Technicians seamlessly integrate the application into their daily work life, allowing it to guide the work that needs to be completed. Administrators use the data collected to make informed decisions about system-wide issues, future planning, and the daily use of technology in the district. Finally, the team is led by an administrator with a forward-thinking vision of where they want to take the district and the department. Decisions are made thoughtfully and proactively when possible. This leader understands how a technology director's role continues to change as a students' access to devices and information increases.

As I write these last thoughts, I have just finished re-reading every page of what I have written over the past several months. I have been reflecting on what I have learned after seventeen years in the education technology arena. One trend with truly successful technology directors that I have observed seems to transcend the district's size, student demographic, financial standing, or location. Successful directors look at how their decisions affect the district stakeholders, not just their department. They make student centered choices. Excellent directors are leaders, not dictators. Allies, not arguments. Bridges, not barriers.

To echo what Mr. Murray said at the start of this text: How will you lead? The choice is up to you.

ABOUT THE AUTHOR

Mike Daugherty is a certified educational technology leader (CETL®) who has served in a variety of roles through his twenty year career in public education. He has found success as a support technician, network administrator, consultant, and an integrationist. In his most recent role as Director of Technology at suburban district near Cleveland, Mike and his team have implemented a highly successful, nationally recognized 1:1 Chromebook initiative in all grade levels.

Through his leadership, the district has become a Google Reference District and was the first district in the country to have all of the teaching staff obtain Google Educator Level 1 certification. In June of 2016, Mike was honored to become a certified Google Innovator with his project focused on helping parents connect to their students' digital lives. His success as a technology director comes from developing creative, well thought out solutions that positively impact teaching and learning. He is currently serving as the Chair of the Learn 21 Ohio Chapter of CoSN. This first book, Modern Edtech Leadership, was originally published in 2015. He published his second book, Certified Edtech Leadership, in 2020. It is available on Amazon.com (https://bit.ly/CertEdTech).

He is supported by his wife Megan and three young children.

Made in the USA
Columbia, SC
09 May 2021